Dancing With Bears

SEPARATING WALL STREET FROM THE BULL

Edward M. Yanis

Writers Club Press
San Jose New York Lincoln Shanghai

Dancing With Bears
Separating Wall Street From The Bull

Published by Writers Club Press
an imprint of iUniverse.com, Inc.

For information address:
iUniverse.com, Inc.
620 North 48th Street
Suite 201
Lincoln, NE 68504-3467
www.iuniverse.com

ISBN: 0-595-00580-2

Printed in the United States of America

*T*o Judy and my beta team.

Epigraph

To make superior profits in the stock market, use the "Y-Process®," a mathematical formula for market timing and risk management. These are more important than security selection.

Contents

Preface

About this book. Dancing With Bears is a book about personal finance, preservation of capital, security selection, market timing and retiring wealthy. The cornerstone of this book is based on a newly developed technology called the *Y-Process*. Simply stated, the Y-Process is a mathematical model that forecasts the risk-reward ratio of any equity portfolio. Based on this forecast, a Y-Process managed portfolio will alert the investor one-week in advance of whether to buy hold or sell their stock. In essence, this is the market timing aspect of this technology.

The Y-Process has been validated by backtesting stock market benchmarks for the last 70 years. The benchmark selected is the one most professional money manager use, that is, the S&P 500 Composite-Stock Index. The results of backtesting are truly startling. An investor using the Y-Process 1) beat the market 66 out of the last 70 years, 2) *never* had a losing year (there were 16 S&P 500 loosing years), and, 3) for the year ending in 1998, had a 40 year annualized return of 18.8 percent versus 8.7 percent for the S&P.

In addition to consistently beating the market, an additional key reason an investor should master this powerful technology is that the Y-Process removes emotions in decisions required of market investors. The factual data that support the validity of the process, and straightforward formulas allow the process to be useful to experienced and novice investors alike.

Acknowledgements

This book in not merely a chapter in my life, but the culmination of a lifetime dream. I owe a tremendous debt of gratitude to all those people who, often in unforeseen way, made the completion of this book possible. Life is very short, and I am aware that, if you are lucky, the opportunity to thank the people who have had a positive influence on your life may come only once. For me, this is it. This is a rare chance for me to reflect back on my life and to express my appreciation to those who helped me reach this point.

First, on a professional note, I want to thank my "red-team" reviewers, an eclectic group of friends at Lockheed Martin, who accepted the challenge of being a red-team member. At that stage, Dancing With Bears was only a group of briefing papers built around the concept of the Y-Process. It was the suggestions of Paul Palosky, Sal Chowdhury, John Corbett, and Lee Fleisher that provided comments on areas that needed additional investigation and evaluation to make the book more appropriate for the average investor.

I would like to thank my editorial team of Bill Waddington, Lee Fleisher and Mike Oliver for all their help and guidance in making this book possible, for having faith in me and my abilities, and for trusting and supporting my challenge of the veracity of the securely established "efficient market theory."

In addition, I thank those people who were my "Beta" Group. To Harrison Frank, Charles Pruzansky, Rita Teicher and Mona Berman who had faith in the Y-Process and invested their hard-earned money in the market for three years using the Y-Process as their market timing tool. By so doing, they verified the Y-Process' outstanding utility for providing superior financial growth and protection against prolonged declines in stock prices. Your payoff was your financial success and my payoff was your letters of thanks and endorsement.

I also owe a debt of gratitude to Joel Parker, Public Relations, who first encouraged me years ago to write a book and to his wife and partner Charlotte, who provided me with the three words that established my writing style—"keep it simple."

On a personal level, I must thank my best friend and wife Judith, who edited drafts of the chapters, and shared in the disappointment of book agent responses, as well as the excitement, labor and tension of this project...and still had encouraging words to offer. To Judy...my heartfelt thanks.

Introduction

NEW INSIGHTS INTO BUILDING WEALTH BY MANAGING YOUR INVESTMENT RISKS.
INVESTORS DON'T NEED A BULL MARKET TO MAKE MONEY.

Few financial endeavors have been written about, diagnosed, or have occupied the time of stock market investors with less success than the attempt to "beat the market." For thiry-five years I have pursued this dream. Most Wall Street professionals claim that few investors can beat the market consistently. This view is supported by modern finance theory and is taught by academia in the nation's leading business schools. It seemed that I was doomed to pursue a dream that could never be realized.

However, in 1986, while doing research on techniques for moderating investment risk, I stumbled across some dramatic statistics. For the 25 years from 1970 through 1994, the Dow Jones Industrial Average (the DJIA Index is the world's most used indicator of U.S. stock market trends) advanced 475%, an increase of almost six-fold over 6318 trading days. When I removed the 75 days contributing to the largest positive cumulative *gains*, I found that the DJIA had a *loss* of 51%; the original DJIA index value dropped by half.

The most astonishing part of the data reveals that when the 75 days contributing the largest *negative* amounts are removed—the advance jumps to 5,200%, an *increase* of 53-fold over the original amount. Upon further research, I discovered that these conclusions apply equally as well to stock market statistics that date back to the 1930s.

Until recently, it has been difficult to apply financial findings such as these to guide current investments, to enhance returns, reduce risk and anticipate downturns. The key to the development of *accurate* and *consistent* "precursors" to market downturns has been to apply computer processing to a mathematical solution I call the "Y-Process." Up to now, there hasn't been the availability of high-power personal computers (at an affordable cost) and the modern computer processing technology required to solve these esoteric mathematical problems.

How The Y-Process Can Be Used To Increase Returns By Reducing Risk. The Y-Process has universal application for all stock portfolios. I empirically tested it against various types of securities, both domestic and international—including stocks, mutual funds, index funds and "index stocks." In *every* test case, it provided the desired results—lowered investor risk and enhanced returns.

To test the accuracy and consistency of the Y-Process, I backtested the Standard and Poor's 500 Composite-stock Index with and without the Y-Process over the past 70-years. The S&P 500 was chosen because it is generally accepted by Wall Street as the "benchmark" for the U. S. stock market. The results: Over the past 70 years, an *unmanaged* S&P 500 investment (buying once and holding onto your purchase) resulted in 22 years of negative returns. On the other hand, with a *Y-Process managed* S&P 500 index—buying and selling the index using the Y-Process' simple formula—there *wasn't* **a loss in any of the 70 years.** The significance of these results cannot be overstated.

A second test also produced similar outstanding results. It was a comparison of the S&P 500 *cumulative* returns with a single buy-and-hold (unmanaged) investment and with a single buy Y-Process managed investment. The table below provides the results for the last four decades.

Years, in Decades	Single Buy-and-Hold Investment in the S&P 500 (Cumulative Returns)	Y-Process Managed Single Investment in the S&P 500 (Cumulative Returns)
Last 10 years (1988-1998)	5-fold	7-fold
Last 20 years (1978-1998)	13-fold	61-fold
Last 30 years (1968-1998)	13-fold	280-fold
Last 40 years (1958-1998)	31-fold	1,155-fold

For each of the 10-year periods shown, a buy-and-hold strategy is not the best approach to achieve superior returns. Why? If you invested in the S&P 500 20 years ago—applying the Y-Process—you would have gained an outstanding return of 61-times your original investment versus a return of only 13-times using a buy-and-hold strategy. If you had invested 30 years ago using the Y-Process, your net worth would have increased 280-times your original investment versus 13-times using a buy-and-hold strategy. Moreover, in each of the decades illustrated, the Y-Process provided the investor an average *42 percent less risk* than the buy-and-hold strategy.

In this book, risk is defined as the percentage of time over the year that you are in the stock market. Being riskless is defined as the percent of time you are invested in U.S. Treasury bills or bonds. For example, if during the year, you are invested in an equity mutual fund or stocks for 30 weeks and one day, then you are at risk (30.2/52)*100 or 58.1 percent. The complement of this is the percentage of time you are "riskless" or 100-58.1=41.9 percent.

Special Features. *Dancing With Bears* is a serious, down-to-earth, easy-to-read educational commentary on stock market investing. It contains chapter subtitles and paragraph subheads that have visual appeal with the inclusion of exercises, checklists, tables, charts and graphs. Where necessary, footnotes are included to clarify some of the detail. Endnotes are used only for references. A glossary is included which will help the reader to easily locate financial and technical terms used throughout the book.

Benefits For Investors. The Y-Process provides investors a tool to help them achieve their financial goals. This book divulges publicly, for the first time, the mathematical solution of the Y-Process for personal use. Now, investors will be able to follow the Y-Process' derivation and its solution to their own stock portfolio. The *Process* furnishes investors the ability to reliably and consistently call major market turns—allowing them to take conservative measures in a timely fashion. In essence, investors will now be able to take total control of their portfolio using this unique risk reduction management tool to: 1) beat the market, 2) enhance returns, and 3) incur less risk.

Chapter 9 contains the Y-Process formula. To assist the reader to verify your stock or fund Y-Process calculations, I provide you technical assistance if you go to my Y-Process web-site. You can view selected market indexes, funds and stocks by logging on to the web-site. At the back of this book (after the glossary) you will find a postal card. If you follow the directions and mail the card to me, I will provide you 13 free weeks of technical support for the aforementioned selected market indexes, fund and stocks. This should give you sufficient confidence that you are performing the Y-Process calculations correctly.

This Book Is Written For Three Levels Of Investors.

Part one. Chapters 1 through 3 are written for the **novice** investor. The objective is to introduce those persons, making their first venture into the stock market, to the language, tools, techniques and investment knowledge to take charge of their financial future. It walks the investor through important investment principles, concepts and strategies. Worksheets are provided to: 1) help the investor establish an understanding of their risk tolerance, 2) assist them to determine their financial status, and 3) define their short, intermediate and long term goals.

Part two. Chapters 4 through 7, focuses on the **intermediate** investor. It takes these investors to the next level of understanding. The objective is to help the informed, risk-sensitive investor to become a more effective manager of their portfolio, with renewed confidence in making risk-reward decisions.

Part three. Chapters 8 through 12 are written for the **sophisticated** investor. These chapters describe the conceptual development, testing and verification of the Y-Process. The objective is to demonstrate how the Y-Process can be used as another important tool in the investor's tool kit—possibly the only tool with a 58% risk reduction* capability and a 97% confidence factor** of outperforming the market. Suggestion: For sophisticated investors who are anxious to use the Y-Pocess, go to Part three, learn the Y-Process and apply it to your portfolio now.

Two New Disclosures In The World Of Investing. This book discloses, for the first time in Chapter 10, a significant finical revelation, a new "efficient-market theory" *form*. This form will affect the way economics and finance academia teach investment and business courses leading to Master of Business Administration (MBA) degrees, Certified Financial Planner (CFP) certification and Certified Financial Analyst (CFA) certification.

The second disclosure is a new anomaly to the efficient-market theory (described in Chapter 10). Efficient-market theory anomalies are not unique; there are six existing today. **The last one was discovered in 1972.**

---

* The 58% risk reduction is the mean value for the last 70 years—1930 through 1999.

** This excludes 10 ties in the 70 years. A tie is less than ± 1.5% difference beetween the Y-Processed managed S&P 500 and its benchmark. This number changes to 93% if ties are included.

PART ONE

—THE NOVICE INVESTOR'S FIRST VENTURE INTO THE STOCK MARKET

(Chapters 1 through 3)

Part One is written for the *novice* investor. The objective is to introduce those persons making their first venture into the stock market, to the language, tools, techniques and investment knowledge to take charge of their financial future. It walks the reader through important investment principles, concepts and strategies. Worksheets are provided to establish risk tolerance; they also assist the reader in determining their financial status, and defining short, intermediate and long term goals.

1

Accumulating Wealth Begins
With Six Simple Tenets

A Financial Checkup Will Prepare You To Take The Steps Required To Establish And Attain Your Financial Expectations.

Taking Control Of Your Financial Future. The time has come to talk sense about the long journey you are about to undertake to take control of your financial future. Building personal wealth starts with these six simple tenets. I created a "memory jogger" for these tenets: "**Go in** the **di**rection of high **ri**sk **in**vestments and in **ti**me you will lose your money and miss great **op**portunities." This is a "hybrid" anagram that contains six two-letter combinations (in bold print). The reader is challenged to match this anagram to the tenets below:

• **One: Set specific financial goals.** The goals you choose affect your investment choices. There are no "right" or "wrong" investment goals. They can be whatever you want them to be. Your income, job security, and your ability to take risks, your age and your financial prospects will influence them.

• **Two: Develop the habit of investing.** The best chance to acquire measurable wealth lies in developing the habit of stashing away a fixed amount on a regular basis and investing the money where it can do the most for you. If you're in a hurry this book won't help you. Buy a lottery ticket instead. But if you're patient, I will show you how to accumulate a six- or seven-figure chunk of money while you still have enough lifetime left to enjoy it. Obtaining wealth this way takes you on a trip that's short on thrills, but it's also short on spills.

• **Three: Diversify your investments.** No investment performs well all the time; as a rule, when something is down, something else tends to be up. One way to protect yourself is to diversify. It's common sense not to put all your eggs in one basket. Some investment experts believe that you can actually increase your returns with a sensible diversification strategy.

• **Four: Invest within your risk tolerance.** Investing requires taking some risks. You can undertake a successful investment strategy by quantifying how much risk you are willing to take. Your hope for investment success depends in part on your ability to reduce those risks without passing up reasonable rewards. And, as I will teach you in Part Three, there are ways to lower your risks.

• **Five: Understand the time-value of money.** The time you have to achieve your goals will influence the kinds of investments you might consider. The reason is rooted in a concept called the *time-value of money* and its close cousin, *opportunity-cost*. Becoming a successful investor often lies in being able to identify the winning side of the time-value equation. You will also learn that reasonable rewards, over time, will be enough to generate the wealth you seek.

• **Six: Understand the meaning of opportunity-cost; the first cousin of the time-value of money.** When you miss an opportunity for obtaining a realistic rate of return on your investment it is at a cost of meeting your financial goals. The opportunity-cost of not receiving money today is the interest (return) you forfeit when the dollars are received in the future rather than today. Or stating it another way, opportunity-cost is the cost of doing one thing and not another. To be an alert investor or buyer, ask yourself before you make any investment or spending choice: "What *else* could I do with the money?" There is one other caution if you tend to be a procrastinator. Not investing present dollars always involves a cost; the cost is the loss of an opportunity to earn a realistic return on these dollars. Thus, *it is better to invest a dollar today than to invest that same dollar in the future or, worse yet, not to invest it at all.*

Each of these tenets will be amplified in turn:

One: Goal-Setting. Investment goal setting is an intensely personal affair that will be guided by your own personal style and preferences. However, there is one thing about setting financial goals: The clarity with which you can envision your investment goals makes a big difference in whether you can apply the discipline to reach them. If you can decide where you want to go and when you want to get there, you *can* get there; it depends on two critical items. First, the time you have to achieve your goals, and second, where and how much of your money to allocate to various types of investments. Here are two examples:

• **College tuition.** Estimate the amount you'll need for your children. Then subtract the amount you believe you'll be able to pay from your projected salary at the time they're in college and any loans or scholarships you think you can rely on. Don't let the projections of $200,000 or more for college tuition in fifteen years scare you off. Save all you can and expect that both you and your child will be able to earn and borrow more.

• **Retirement.** How much will you need to supplement Social Security and pension payment—and to give yourself a comfortable lead over inflation? A good rule of thumb: seek retirement income (including Social Security, pensions, income from investments, etc.) to at least equal 70 percent of your current income. This assumes that your medical insurance, e.g., Medicare, keeps up with the cost of medical care.

Don't underestimate how much money you will earn on your retirement savings after you retire. Remember, after retirement you will have more time to attend to your investment strategies and by that time you should be an experienced investor using the Y-Process to reduce your risk and enhance your returns. To a large extent, these earnings can still be tax-deferred until you withdraw them. And your tax bracket could well be less—but don't count on it.

• **Where do you stand now?** The first thing you should do is determine the state of your financial health. I have prepared two work sheets that lay the necessary groundwork for setting your investment goals and making plans to reach them. These worksheets allow you to establish your financial baseline and they will assist you in starting your investment program. I suggest that you make copies so that you can use them annually to update the status of your financial health. Worksheet 1.1, "Your Personal Balance Sheet", allows you to determine what type of financial condition you're in. Use this worksheet to calculate current assets, liabilities and net worth. When you know the source of your current net worth, you can determine the strength and weakness of your financial position.

Worksheet 1.2, "How Are Your Investments Deployed?" allows you to determine the status of your investment mix. Complete this worksheet at least once a year so you'll know how your investment mix is changing and can take action, if necessary, to bring it back into line with a mix that matches your goals and your risk tolerance.

Worksheet 1.1 Your Personal Balance Sheet Tells You Where You Stand Now.

ASSETS		LIABILITIES	
Cash on hand	$	Balanced owed on mortgage	$
Savings accounts		Auto loans	
Checking accounts		Student Loans	
Certificate of deposit		Home-equity credit line	
Money-market funds		Other credit lines	
Savings bonds		Credit card bills due	
Market value of home		Other outstanding bills	
Market value of other real estate		**Total Liabilities**	
Cash value of life insurance		**Current Net Worth** (Date:)	$
		(Total Assets minus Total Liabilities)	
Surrender value of annuities			
Vested equity in pension plans			
Vested equity in profit sharing			
Roth, 401(k), or 403(b) plans			
Individual Retirement Accounts			
Keogh plans			
Stocks owned			
Bonds owned			
REITs owned			
Equity mutual funds: (list separately)			
Bond mutual funds:			
Estimated value of other investments:			
Collectibles			
Precious metals			
Antiques			
Household furnishings			
Silverware			
Automobiles and trucks			
Boats, planes, recreational vehicles			
Furs and jewelry			
Loans owed you			
Other assets			
Total Assets	$		

Worksheet 1.2 How Are Your Investments Allocated?

	MARKET VALUE	PERCENT OF TOTAL
CASH		
Savings accounts		
Money-market funds		
Treasury bills		
Total Cash	$	
STOCKS		
Individual shares		
Mutual funds		
Total Stocks	$	
BONDS		
Individual bonds		
Mutual funds		
Unit trusts		
Total Bonds	$	
RENTAL REAL ESTATE	$	
LIMITED PARTNERSHIPS	$	
PRECIOUS METALS	$	
OTHER INVESTMENTS	$	
COLECTIBLES	$	
Total Investments	$	100%

• **Most people have several goals at once.** These can be separated into short-, intermediate- and long-term goals. Your goals are likely to change, so it's important to reassess them from time to time. For instance, the kinds of growth oriented investments that might be perfectly appropriate while you are accumulating a retirement nest egg and have a long-term horizon could be inappropriate after you retire and need part of your investments as income to pay the bills. Under these circumstances, the investment universe is so vast—not just stocks, mutual funds, bonds and certificates, but also hybrids too numerous to mention here—that you'll never be at a loss for choices. Let's examine each of these three types of goals.

• **Short-term goals.** Suppose, for instance, that a cruise to Alaska is one of your goals and that you want to go next summer. Such a short time horizon suggests that the stock market wouldn't be a good place to invest the money you're setting aside for the trip. The market is subject to wide swings, and you wouldn't want to be forced to sell your stocks in a down-swing just because the time had come to buy your tickets. Don't put any money into the stock market that you think you might need in the next three to five years. Where to invest your money? Certificates of deposit that mature about the time you'll need the cash, or a money-market fund that allows you to withdraw your cash instantly by writing a check would be a better choice for this goal.

• **Intermediate-term goals.** Maybe you'd like to buy a larger house within three or five years. With more time, you have more flexibility. Safety is still important but you are in a better position to ride out bad times in the financial markets. For intermediate-term goals like these, you should consider long-term CDs that pay more interest than the short-term certificates you would buy to help finance your cruise. You could even consider mutual funds that invest in stocks that pay good dividends but don't tend to fluctuate much in price That would give you high income (for reinvesting in more fund shares), a chance to ride along if the stock market zooms, and pretty good protection against all but a catastrophic drop in stock prices. But in Part Three, I will teach you a strategy to protect yourself even against this type of market meltdown condition.

• **Long-term goals.** Ah, here's the real wealth-building opportunity. Wise investors have always known that those who have risen to great wealth from humble beginnings had a long-term perspective. Interestingly, the truly rich seem to come from one of two categories: first, the hard working entrepreneur who learns early to reinvest in their business; and second, the serious employee who never seemed to have a penny to spend but moves to a grand home in Arizona or North Carolina five years before the rest of us retire.

A comfortable retirement is probably the most common of all financial goals. A college education for the kids is another common goal. For long-term goals like these, consider a wide range of possibilities: stocks, corporate and government bonds, and long-term CDs among them. You should also take maximum advantage of tax-sheltered plans, such as, individual retirement accounts (IRAs), in which earnings accumulate tax-free and contributions to which may be tax deductible, self employment plans (SEPs) if applicable, or 401(K) plans offered by your employer, which provide many of the same advantages as IRAs.

With several years and sometimes decades ahead of you, financial assets that aren't strictly investments also come into play: home equity, pension plans and social security, for example. The size and accessibility of those assets should influence your investment goals and choices.

Two: Make Investing A Regular Habit. As a new investor, your task is to create a plan that suits you and stick with it. For most people who start with a small amount of money, the best chance to acquire measurable wealth is the same way a marathoner trains for long distance races. The marathoner starts with a plan to run 26.2 miles. They build their body muscles and endurance by following a strict training program using a continuous and rhythmic running style. As a long-term investor, you should develop a similar type of style. Develop the habit of putting money into an account (where it does most good for you) on a consistent and regular interval. The rewards can be considerable. Here are some examples.

Suppose you take $5,000 and put it in the bank, where it earns a nice, safe, sedate 5.5% interest. Twenty years later you come in to claim your deposit and discover that it has grown to a not very impressive $14,500. This is no miracle but it does indicate the possibilities of compounding.

Meanwhile, your sister-in-law has developed the habit of investing on a *consistent and regular basis.* She socks-away $5,000 in one-year certificates of deposit (CDs), at the same bank, with instructions to roll over the proceeds into a new certificate every 12 months. In addition, every month she buys another CD for $100 and issues the same instructions. Over 20 years she earns an average of 8% interest. Her nest egg: more than $80,000. Now this illustrates two important tenets. First, the habit of investing, and second, the time-value of money, sometimes referred to as the miracle of compounding!

Although this is a lot better, it's not going to finance a worry-free retirement. Suppose, as a novice investor, your goal is a lot loftier than that? Suppose you'd like to have a nest egg of half-a-million dollars? You've got 20 years to get there and $5,000 with which to start. With time, experience and learning, you will become a sophisticated investor by investigating in alternatives that should boost your return above what you'd earn in a bank account. What's a reasonable return to plan on and how much will you have to contribute along the way?

For reasons you'll find discussed in Chapter 10 on A Y-Process Managed S&P 500 Consistently Outperforms The Market, I believe an average annual return of greater than 15% over the long run is a reasonable expectation for individuals who apply the principles laid out in this book. At that rate, with $5,000 to start, you'll reach your $500,000 goal if you contribute an additional $320 a month to your investment account.

Less ambitious plans can also work wonders. Starting from zero, putting just $50 a month into an investment that pays a compounded average annual total return of 15% for 20 years will get you a nest egg of better than $65,000. Stick to the plan for 30 years and you'll have more than $275,000. Double your contribution and you'll double the size of your nest egg. For a look at the results of a variety of regular investment amounts earning different rates of return, see *Useful Numbers Every Investor Can Use* in Appendix A and B.

Starting small and gradually increasing your monthly investment amount as your income grows is another possibility. For instance, you can start with no initial investments, put $100 a month into your investment account for five years, raise it to $200 a month for the next five, $300 a month for years 11 through 15 and $400 a month for years 16 through 20. At the end of the period you'll have nearly $227,000. Boost your monthly amount to $500 for years 21 through 25 and your fund will grow to almost $500,000, assuming you earn an average of 15% per year.

How common is an average annual return of 15%. For the 10-year period through 1999, no fewer than 45 different mutual funds delivered that much or more. You'll find most of them listed in many periodicals including *Mutual Funds* magazine, along with lists of other outstanding funds that can help you achieve your goals. Were the 1990s typical for investors? No, they weren't. The Dow Jones Industrial Average quadrupled during the decade—a remarkable performance, though not unique, ending the decade in the neighborhood of 11,500. The Dow also tripled in the ten-year span from 1942 to 1952, and again from 1953 to 1963. In the decade of the 1990s the Dow and the S&P 500 essentially ended the decade in a virtual tie at 317 percent. But helping you achieve mediocre investment results isn't the goal of this book. If you follow the Y-Process strategy, you should do better than that.

These examples are oversimplified, of course, because they don't take taxes or commissions into account. But the point is the same: It validates investing's first simple truth—making investing a regular habit is your best chance to acquire measurable wealth.

Three: Diversify Your Investments. There are at least three good reasons to diversify your investments. First, it's common sense not to put all your eggs in one basket unless you like omelets. Our mothers taught us that. Second, no investment performs well all the time; as a rule, when something is down, something else tends to be up. And third, diversification allows you to sleep peacefully at night.

• **Spreading the risk.** One way to hedge your bets is to select a number of investment vehicles you like and divide your money equally among them. Some investment advisors recommend investing an equal amount in a five-part "fixed mix" portfolio consisting of cash (money-market funds, CDs, Treasury bills); bonds; U.S. stocks; foreign stocks; and real estate. Once a year, adjust the mix to maintain the dollar balance. You do that by taking the gains from the winners and spreading them out among the losers so that your asset distribution stays the same. Other than that, sit back and forget it.

For example, if you had stuck with this fixed-mix approach from 1965 to 1990, and your selection of stocks, bonds and real estate had matched the average market experience for those investments, your cumulative return would have been a shade under 950%. Looked at another way, $1,000 invested in 1965 would have grown to $9,500 by 1990. The same amount invested in U.S. stocks would have grown to about $8,700 measured by the Standard & Poor's 500 Composite Index. The most spectacular returns during that period came from a portfolio of international stocks, which rocketed a phenomenal 2,477%, turning $1,000 into $24,770.

The results work out to an average annual return of 10.2% for the diversified portfolio over 25 years. That's not bad, but its not much better than the historical return generated by the stock market alone.

• **Another approach: The 40-40-20 portfolio.** Dividing your portfolio equally among domestic stocks, foreign stocks, bonds, real estate and cash equivalents is only one approach to diversification. Another formula, which is popular with many successful investors seeking to prosper while controlling their risks, is the 40-40-20 portfolio: 40% in stocks, 40% in bonds and 20% in cash equivalents. Either mix creates a good diversified portfolio, but thinking about a portfolio in such terms can lure you into a misleading sense of permanence about what is actually a very fluid situation. As stock prices and interest rates go up and down, the proportions in your portfolio will shift without your lifting a finger. In addition, there will be times when you want to shift more money into stocks or bonds or cash, for reasons described in Chapters 2 and 12. It is more realistic to think in terms of ranges rather than fixed percentages. Use the Worksheets 1.1 and 1.2 to discover how your investments sort out today. The results will suggest moves you should make to get them more in line with the kind of proportion you'd like.

• **How well did various types of investments perform over the years?** Table 1.0 is a snapshot of selected recent years of stocks, bonds, Treasury bills, gold and real estate investments and the inflation value for those years. The investment figures are total returns, which means they include price changes and assume that all earnings from the investment, if any, are reinvested. They should all be compared to inflation figures for those years because inflation is a source of risk. If prices of goods and services increase, the real purchasing power of your assets and the income generated by them is reduced. Inflation erodes the buying power of your assets and income.

Stocks and money-market funds managed positive returns in each of the six years. Two highly touted investments—gold and real estate-soared, struggled or nearly collapsed, depending on the year that you're looking at. A different selection of years would have shown a different pattern from the ones shown above.

Table 1.0. Comparison of inflation and various investments types over the last three decades.

Year		1975	1979	1985	1989	1995	1999
Inflation rate, %=		6.9	13.3	3.8	4.6	2.8	2.1
Dow Jones industrials	(rate of return, %)	44.8	10.6	33.6	32.2	33.5	25.2
Long-term Treasuries	(rate of return, %)	8.3	-0.5	31.6	18.9	-22.9	5.9
Money Market Index	(rate of return, %)	NA	12.8	7.2	8.9	5.5	4.5
Gold	(rate of return, %)	-24.9	126.6	6.9	-2	2.3	0.4
Real Estate Investment	(rate of return, %)	27.3	18.3	0.8	-21.9	7.4	NA

Source: Statistical Abstract of the United States—The National Data Book, for years shown. Each of the five-year intervals starts on January 1 and ends on December 31.

For instance, even with dividends included, the Dow Jones industrials turned in a dismal performance in 1973, 1974 and 1977. Gold soared in each of those years, while real estate investment trusts fell so sharply in 1973 and 1974 that their survival as an investment vehicle was actually in doubt.

The lesson here isn't hard to find; invest in whatever you want, but invest in something else, too. There is another message in this table as well. In the selected years shown, only the stock market index as represented by the Dow Jones Industrial Average had only positive years and beat inflation in each year except in 1979.

• **Another approach to diversification using the "Modern Portfolio Theory."** Notwithstanding this common sense assessment of diversification across many types of investments as shown in the above table, there are additional ways that investors can sleep more soundly every night. Thanks to Harry M. Markowitz, who is known as the father of Modern Portfolio Theory (MPT), brought mathematics up to common sense and revolutionized the world of finance in 1950. The MPT brought the scientific approach to risk by encouraging investors to diversify by investing in assets that perform differently from one another. The MPT downplays the talents of the stock picker and emphasizes the chef-like importance of mixing the right ingredients into the mix. The insight Markowitz offered was how to make the most money with the least amount of risk.

With time and additional investment experience, the novice investor will move on to a higher level of investing skill. When you reach the sophisticated level, you will learn how to use the MPT in conjunction with the Y-Process to optimize your stock market returns at reduced risk.

Four: How Risk Shy Are You? Some finance books on investment define risk as: The chance you take that you will earn less from an investment than the rate of inflation or less than the interest available at the time from insured savings certificates or U.S. Treasury-backed obligations.

But if you ask most people what they consider as risk they would say: "Risk is the chance that you will lose all or part of the money you have invested." That's true as far as it goes, but it doesn't go far enough. A more complete definition of risk acknowledges the availability of investments carrying virtually iron-clad guarantees that you will get all your money back plus the interest promised you: savings accounts in federally insured banks, savings and loans, or credit unions, for instance. These are and will remain safe despite the past problems of some institutions and the fund that insures their deposits. Also, with all investments, even government-guaranteed ones, you run the risk that your rate of return will be less than the inflation rate.

In fact, savings accounts, certificates of deposit, Treasury bills, savings bonds and a handful of other government-backed investments establish a useful benchmark for measuring risk.

• **Establish your risk zone.** It's difficult to pick up a book on investing without running into something called the pyramid of risk, and this book will be no exception. The pyramid is built on a broad and solid base of financial security: a home; money salted away in insured savings accounts or certificates; plus insurance policies to cover your health, your car, your home, your life and your ability to earn an income (that is, disability insurance). As you move up from the pyramid's base, the levels get narrower and narrower, representing the space in your portfolio that is available for investments that involve risk. The greater the risks of an investment, the higher up the pyramid it goes and, thus, the less money you should put into it.

The image itself is more important than some of the specifics of what belongs on each level of the pyramid. Weak real estate markets in some places in recent years have raised the question of whether home ownership still belongs at the base of the pyramid. I believe that it does for security as much as for wealth.

• **How much should you have in savings?** Three to six months' living expenses should be your goal. Bank, savings and loan or credit union accounts are good places to keep this money, but look for opportunities to earn more than the present 2% or 2 1/2% these institutions tend to pay on their run-of-the-mill deposit accounts. If you can't do better than that in local institutions, consider a money-market fund for at least part of your rainy-day money. Such funds aren't federally insured, but they are prudent, conservative places to put your money and they pay a higher return.

Once you've built the base of your pyramid, you're ready to move up and become an investor. One level up from savings, insurance and home ownership is the appropriate place for mutual funds that invest in low-risk, dividend-oriented stocks and top-quality government and corporate bonds. Individual stocks and bonds that you pick yourself are on the same level. Most experts would put investment real estate on the next level up from stocks. At the very top of the pyramid go investments few people should try, such as penny stocks, commodities futures contracts and most limited partnerships.

Thus, the pyramid, which is broad and solid at the bottom and gets narrower and smaller as you move up, is the perfect image for the sensible deployment of your financial resources. As long as you remember that, you'll never stray too far out of your risk zone.

• **Establish your risk comfort level.** Everyone has a level at which the loss of a certain amount of money causes them pain or discomfort. If you lose less than this value, you're still in your risk comfort level. If you lose more than this amount then you have established your loss aversion value. Certainly you should never invest in something that makes you uncomfortable or in something you don't understand or invest in someone's tip without doing your homework. It is well known that too many investors seem perfectly comfortable with entirely too much risk until the market goes into free-fall. The signs are there if you are honest with yourself. If you are constantly concerned or lose sleep when your investment turns down, these are indicators that you are over your risk comfort level. This is not a good position for you to be in.

Included at the end of this chapter, is a risk exam that will tell you what type of investor you are—conservative, active or venturesome. If you are too venturesome, the remedy is obvious. Scale-back and or move your investments into less risky ventures and above all do not margin your stocks, that is, don't buy stocks with borrowed money.

• **The risk-reward relationship.** In all financial ventures, a risk-reward relationship applies, no matter what the investment, the reputation of the investment adviser, or the financial condition of the market. The landscape is littered with forlorn investors who forgot this basic fact: The risk you take should be commensurate with your expected return. Conversely, the bigger the promised reward, the bigger the risk.

Does this mean you should avoid all high-risk investments? No. It means you should only invest as much as you can afford to lose, because there is a good chance you *will* lose it. You should also learn to recognize the risks involved in every kind of investment. And above all, stay within your risk comfort level.

• **What is a prudent risk?** It depends on your goals, your age, your income and other resources and your current and future financial obligations. A young single person who expects their pay to rise steadily over the years and who has few family responsibilities can afford to take more chances than, say, a couple approaching retirement age. The young person has time to recover from market reversals; the older couple may not.

• **Risks in stocks.** A company's stock may decline in price because its business climate is unfavorable, or the company hits the skids for whatever exogenous reason, or isn't being managed well and the shareholders lose faith. It may also decline in price because large numbers of investors decide to move into bonds or cash on a particular day and sell millions of shares of stock of all kinds. This behavior drives the market price down and takes dozens of companies along without bothering to differentiate the good from the bad.

• **Risks in bonds.** Bond prices tend to move in the opposite direction from interest rates, rising in price when rates fall and vice versa. But individual bond issues can be hurt even if interest rates in general are falling. All it takes is for one of the rating services, Standard and Poor's and Moody's are the major ones, to downgrade its opinion of the company's financial stability. A bond issue that's paying an interest rate noticeably higher than that of other bonds with a similar maturity date is probably forced to pay it to compensate investors for the higher risk inherent in a lower safety rating. That, in a nutshell, is the situation with "junk" bonds: low ratings, high interest, and high risk of default.

• **Risks everywhere.** Real estate values go up and down in synchronism with supply and demand in *local* markets, regardless of the health of the national economy. Gold and silver, which are supposed to be stores of value in inflationary times, have been decidedly unrewarding in times of tolerable inflation. Even federally insured savings accounts carry risks, not that the government won't cover insured deposits, but that their low interest rate won't be enough to protect the value of your money from the combined effect of inflation and taxes.

Five: Apply The "Time-Value Of Money" Concept To Your Investment Strategy. An easy way to remember what the *time-value of money* really means is to reverse the phrase to *money's value in time*.

The time-value of money concept is crucial in financial planning because the value of money changes with time. The value of a dollar today is not equal to the value of that same dollar tomorrow. Now, if that doesn't make sense, let me explain why. A dollar today is worth more than a dollar expected at some future time because a dollar today can be invested to earn interest leading to an increase in your wealth. This concept is probably the source of an old Indian proverb: *A bird in the hand is worth two in the bush.*

Which would you rather have, $1000 today or $1000 a year from today? Of course you'd choose to take the money now—anyone would. You should understand that the value of that $1000 you have today will erode by a year's worth of inflation and a year's worth of lost interest on the money. To put a dollar figure on it, if inflation is 5% and you could earn 7% interest in a year, the thrill of being handed $1000 today is worth about 12%, or $120; that's a lot more than the thrill of being handed $1000 a year from today.

Success with your money often lies in being able to identify the winning side of the time-value equation. The time-value of money works against you if you're the one waiting to collect the money, but it works in your favor if you're the one who has to pay. Here is an example to explain the winning side of the time-value equation.

Let's say you've just won your state's $1-million lottery. You're offered the choice of taking the million-dollars paid out over 20 years or $500,000 paid in cash. Which should you take?

The answer depends on many factors. Strictly from a financial aspect, it depends mostly on what return you could get on your lump sum *after* taxes are paid to the federal and some state governments. If you choose the lump sum, you'd have less than half of the money left (after taxes) or about $230,000. This assumes you are married, filing jointly and that your state tax rate is about 4.5 percent. Assuming what's left of your lump sum can be invested over the next 20 years at 12% per year, you'll be way ahead of the game. In 20 years, the total cumulative return would be $2.2-million. Even if you invested your $230,000 at 7 3/4 % for the next 20 years, you would still exceed the million dollars paid out in the annuity choice. (Remember *money's value in time!*)

It is the time-value of money that permits state governments and other sponsors of sweepstakes and lotteries to promise fabulous payouts that actually exceed the amount of money they take in by selling tickets. Consider two lotteries, both of which promise a million-dollar prize. One pays it right away and the other, which advertises an "annuity value" of a million dollars, pays you $50,000 a year for 20 years. That's a million dollars, all right, but it doesn't cost the lottery sponsor nearly that much. In fact, the sponsor can purchase an annuity contract from an insurance company that will fulfill its obligation for less than half the eventual payout.

Annuities are contracts that pay a certain sum of money in regular installments over a period of time, often 10 or 20 years, rather than in a lump sum. Stretching out the payments creates a big benefit for the state that owes the money because it collects interest on the unpaid amount while the recipient waits to collect. For instance, if the $50,000 were paid out in annual installments stretched over 20 years, and the state earned 7 1/4 % on the unpaid amount, all it would need to meet that schedule of future payments would be about $25,000 today. Thus, your choice of selecting a lump sum in lieu of $50,000 per year would really be no contest. That is, of course, unless you choose to invest your lump sum in a savings account which pays one of the lowest returns of most investments.

For comparison, in the first quarter of 1999, the average taxable money fund yielded 4.4%, and half returned more. That easily beat the insured money market account at banks and thrifts (2.8%) and sixty-day CDs (3.1%). It even matched five-year CDs, which tied up your money for sixty long months and subjected it to early-withdrawal penalties. And it's far above the 1% inflation rate of the 1990s.

Another example of the time-value of money illustrates its worthiness as a goal setting strategy:

• **Paying the kids' college bills.** Your future biomedical engineer faces education costs exceeding $250,000 when they enter Columbia University or Brown in 18 years. That's a huge sum, but because you're familiar with the time-value of money, you know the smart thing to do is to find a way to pay those bills today, when your dollars are worth more than they will be in 18 years. Assuming a time-value for the money of 12% per year (meaning you could earn that much on the money between now and the time you have to pay it) the value of the $250,000 you need 18 years from now is a shade under $32,500 today. Salt those away in an investment earning 12% a year and you have the bills covered. If you haven't got $32,500, gather as much of it as you can and get the time-value of money working for you, easing at least some of the burden when the college bills come due. Or raise your sights a bit. If you could manage to earn 15% on the money, you'd need just slightly over $20,000 today to have $250,000 by your daughter's freshman year. Chapter 10 describes an investment strategy, using the Y-Process, to achieve such a goal.

Six: Opportunity-Cost: The First Cousin Of Time-Value Of Money. An example of opportunity-cost illustrates its worthiness as goal setting strategy. For example, paying off the mortgage. Ignorance of opportunity-cost can cause you to think you're doing something smart when you're not. For instance, you have probably heard praises sung for cutting your mortgage time in half by boosting your monthly mortgage premium payments. Because you pay it off sooner than a 30-year loan, you pay less interest and thus save tens of thousands of dollars. But the homeowner with the 15-year mortgage parts with the money sooner than the 30-year buyer. And you just learned that the time-value of money suggests some caution may be in order before making extravagant claims of savings. You need to answer the following two questions: What else might you do with the extra money you'd be spending on the higher monthly payments required by the 15-year mortgage? How much could it earn if you invested it in something other than mortgage payments?

Suppose it costs you an extra $200 a month to pay off the loan in 15 years instead of 30. That's $200 a month that is not available for something else—investing in a mutual fund, for example. Say the mortgage rate is 7% and the mutual fund earns 9%. You could benefit from that 2% difference by putting the money in the fund instead of paying off the mortgage. $200 a month earning 12% compounded for 15 years grows to almost $42,000. That's your *opportunity-cost* by paying-off your mortgage early. Before you crow about how much you've saved by prepaying your 30-year mortgage, you should subtract your opportunity-cost from your savings.

There is one more important aspect that you should consider in your opportunity-cost equation. Uncle Sam allows you to deduct mortgage interest from your federal taxes. And, depending on your bracket, for every one hundred dollars you deduct, Uncle Sam hands you back $15—$39.

The Donoghue Risk Test.* Unless you've already accumulated a pile of riches, you're likely to find that when you add up all your desires, the total exceeds the amounts you're confident you can accumulate by "first paying yourself" every month and then investing; especially if you aren't yet persuaded that you can achieve investment returns of more than, say, 10 percent a year.

The good news is that you're probably more ready to take an aggressive investing stance than you realize—and with a little bit of discipline using the Y-Process you can probably build that nest egg faster than you expect.

Before you complete the process of negotiating your financial goals with yourself, take the following risk test. It will help you determine what kind of investor you are—and what kind of investor you may want to become:

1. You buy an investment based on the strategies in this book. But a month later, the entire stock market declines and the value of your investment goes down 15 percent. The fundamental reasons why you bought it still seem sound. Do you:

   a—Sit tight and wait for it to go back up?

   b—Sell it and rid yourself of further sleepless nights?

   c—Buy more—if it looked good at the original price it looks even better now?

* Source. William E. Donoghue, *The Donoghue Strategies*, Bantam Books, 1981. p.41

2. Which would you rather have done?

    a—Invested in an "aggressive growth" mutual fund which failed to increase in value over six months.

    b—Invested in a money market fund, only to see an aggressive growth fund you had been thinking about rise 50 percent in value in six months

3. Would you feel better if:

    a—You doubled your money in a stock market mutual fund?

    b—Your money market fund investment saved you from losing half your money in a market slide?

4. Which situation would make you feel happiest?

    a—You win $100,000 in a publisher's contest.

    b—You inherit $100,000 from a rich relative.

    c—You earn $100,000 by risking $2,000 in the options market.

    d—Any of the above—you're happy with the $100,000, no matter where it came from.

5. Your apartment building is being converted to condominiums. You can either buy your unit for $80,000 or sell the option for $20,000. The condo's market value is $120,000. You know that if you bought the condo, it might take six months to sell. The monthly carrying cost would be $1,200, and you'd have to borrow the down payment for a mortgage. You don't want to live in the building. So what do you do?

    a—Take the $20,000.

    b—Buy the unit and then sell it on the open market.

6. You inherit your uncle's $100,000 house, free of any mortgage. Although the house is in a fashionable neighborhood and can be expected to appreciate at a faster rate than inflation, it has deteriorated badly. It would net $1,000 monthly if rented as is; it would net $1,500 per month if renovated. The renovations could be financed by a mortgage on the property. You would:

    a—Sell the house.

    b—Rent it as is.

    c—Make the necessary renovations, then rent it.

7. You work for a small but thriving privately held electronics company. The company is raising money by selling stock to its employees. The managers plan to take the company public, but not for four or more years. If you buy the stock, you will not be allowed to sell until the shares are traded publicly. In the meantime, the stock will pay no dividends. But when the company goes public, the shares could trade for ten or twenty times what you would pay. How much of an investment would you make?

    a—None at all.

    b—One month's salary.

    c—Three months' salary.

    d—Six months' salary.

8. Your cousin, a biologist who has made large profits investing in the stock market, tells you that unusual gains can be expected in the stocks of certain small companies. He recommends a mutual fund that invests in them. You know nothing about publicly traded small companies, but you've heard they are risky investments. What do you do?

a—Invest in the mutual fund immediately based on your cousin's recommendation.

b—Send for the mutual fund's prospectus, and watch the newspaper for information to help you decide whether your cousin's suggestion is correct.

c—Leave your money in a bank or money market mutual fund.

d—Call a stockbroker for advice, and buy shares in IBM when the broker tells you IBM is less risky.

9. Your long-time friend and neighbor, an experienced petroleum geologist, is assembling a group of investors (of which he is one) to fund an exploratory oil well which could pay back fifty to one hundred times its investment if successful. If the well is dry, the entire investment will be worthless. Your friend estimates the chance of success is only 20 percent. What would you invest?

a—Nothing.

b—One month's salary.

c—Three months' salary.

d—Six months' salary.

10. You learn that several commercial real estate developers are considering purchase of undeveloped land in a certain location. You are offered an option to buy a choice parcel. The cost is about two months' salary and you calculate the potential gain to be ten months' salary. Do you:

a—Purchase the option.

b—Let it slide; it's not for you.

11. You are on a TV game show and can choose one of the following. Which would you take?

   a—$1,000 in cash.

   b—A 50 percent chance at winning $4,000.

   c—A 20 percent chance at winning $10,000.

   d—A 5 percent chance at winning $100,000.

12. It's 1992, and inflation is returning. "Hard assets" such as precious metals, collectibles, and real estate are expected to keep pace with inflation. Your assets are now all in long-term bonds. What would you do?

   a—Hold the bonds.

   b—Sell the bonds and put half the proceeds into money funds and the other half into hard assets.

   c—Sell the bonds and put all the proceeds into hard assets.

   d—Sell the bonds, put all the money into hard assets, and borrow additional money to buy more.

• **Scoring:**

Now it's time to see what kind of investor you are. Total your score, using the point system below for each answer you gave.

Your score

___1.	a-3	b-1	c-4	
___2.	a-3	b-1		
___3.	a-2	b-1		
___4.	a-2	b-1	c-4	d-1
___5.	a-1	b-2		
___6.	a-1	b-2	c-3	
___7.	a-1	b-2	c-4	d-6
___8.	a-5	b-3	c-1	d-1
___9.	a-1	b-3	c-6	d-9

___10.   a-3   b-1
___11.   a-1   b-3   c-5   d-9
___12.   a-1   b-2   c-4   d-6

___Total

• **If you scored:**

Below 18: You are a **prudent investor** who tends to take calculated risks but only with solid investments that you believe to be undervalued. Stick with sober, conservative investments until you develop the confidence or desire to adopt more "aggressive" strategies. But when interest rates are falling and a bull market in stocks seems to be starting, don't eliminate the possibility of investing part of your funds in growth mutual funds.

Between 18-32: You are an **active investor** who tends to seek a more balanced approach to risk and return. As an active investor you are willing to take calculated risks to achieve gains. You will consider various investment strategies, and in the long run you'll achieve greater gains.

33 and over: You're an **aggressive investor.** You tend to take bigger risks in anticipation of bigger returns. Remember that the search for more return carries *greater risks.* If, however, you know you will not hit home runs all the time and are willing to strike out once in a while, you might as well get up at the plate and swing for the fences. As you advance in your investing skill level, you will read Part Three. As an advanced aggressive investor, you will learn how to use the Y-Process to enhance your returns while minimizing your risk.

2

For The Prudent Investor Is It Stocks Or Bonds?

BONDS CAN BE SAFE, BUT ONLY IF YOU DON'T NEED THE MONEY.

Stock Versus Bonds Description. For the novice investor, when I write about stock, I'm referring to an investment that means having an ownership certificate of a corporation, i.e., a stock certificate. A bond, on the other hand, is any debt security, such as an "IOU" or a corporation promissory note. The bottom line—stock (or equity) means *ownership* and bonds means *debt*.

Bonds come in a variety of maturities. The long bond is the U.S. government's 30-year bond. Its yield is the one often cited by the media when interest rates are being discussed. Treasury notes have shorter terms, maturing in two, five or ten years. Treasury bills (or T-bills) mature in 13, 26, or 52 weeks. The minimum purchase amount for all of these bills is $1,000.

For The Prudent Investor, Use Yanis' First Principle of Investing: *"Preservation of Capital with Realistic Returns"*. Modern, sophisticated investors, who are willing to develop a well thought-out, sound strategy for managing their investments qualifies as the only truly prudent investors. The key to developing such a strategy is to adopt *Preservation of capital with realistic returns* as your first principle of investing.

Does the preservation of capital mean to invest only in bonds? No. For the average investor, preservation of capital means retaining your principal—the dollar value of your original investment plus any growth. However, preservation of capital is much more complex. Many investors believe that "risk-free" government bonds provide a conservative preservation approach. You'll learn, in this chapter, that investing in bonds has severe limitations. There are better ways to preserve your capital.

What does "realistic returns" mean? Realistic returns are dividends, interest, and capital gains on your investments—accumulating wealth. The stock market has the potential to maximize your wealth. No other investment available to intelligent novice investors with average resources, a willingness to take risks, and a limited amount of time to spend on active management, delivers as well as stocks over the long term. Not real estate, gold, bonds, and certainly not savings accounts.

For the novice investor, it is important to note that as long-term investments, *stocks outperform bonds*. According to Pennsylvania University Professor J. Siegel's book, *Stocks for the Long Run*, from 1802 to 1997 the stock market offered an average nominal annual return of 8.4 percent per year, compared with 4.8 percent for long-term government bonds. From 1926 to 1997, stocks outperformed bonds 10.6 percent to 5.2 percent. From 1966 to 1997, it was 11.5 percent vs. 7.9 percent. Money that you are investing for decades will grow more quickly in the stock market than in bonds.

What Are The "Real Returns" Of Stocks And Bonds?
There is much to be learned from reviewing the history of risk-reward relationships in both the stock and bond markets. Probably the best study of comparative investment

results ever undertaken was performed by Roger Ibbotson* who evaluated records back to 1930. These results are summarized in Table 2.1. Ibbotson calculated the compound annual returns (including reinvested dividends and interest) of the Standard and Poors 500 composite-price index (a proxy for the stock market) and long-term government bonds.

The reader is advised to study Table 2.1 and match the returns of stocks and bonds against each other and against the inflation rate. Ibbotson has two columns for each period studied. The first column contains nominal returns for stocks versus bonds. The second column contains a comparison of inflation-adjusted returns for stocks versus bonds. In every period shown over the 70 years evaluated, stocks outperformed bonds except for the rapid inflationary period (1970-79) where stocks and bonds tied and underperformed the inflation rate. This leads us to a most important topic for investors. Inflation must be taken into account when making investment decisions.

Inflation Can Be Hazardous To Your Financial Wealth.
Inflation erodes the purchasing power of the dollar. However, the real loss that an investor experiences is best understood by an historic comparison of stocks and bonds. Research on returns and inflation over an extended period of time has shown that the "nominal" return on common stocks has exceeded the rate of inflation by about five percent. But this is not the whole story. Table 2.1 shows the long-term results from 1930 through 1998, a period that includes the two biggest stock market crashes** in history, plus the Great Depression. When "nominal" returns are adjusted for inflation***,

---

* Ibbotson's 1996 Year book (modified by the author to update long-term returns to 1998)

** Technically, the first great crash began in Oct. 1929.

*** Inflation-adjusted returns measure the increase in purchasing power earned by the investor. The inflation-adjusted return is determined by the following equation: [(1+ nominal return)/(1+ rate of inflation)-1]*100%. Thus for 1930-98, the inflation-adjusted rate is [(1+. 104)/(1+. 031)-1]*100%= 7.0805%=7.1% (rounded).

as they are in the table, inflation-adjusted returns (sometimes-called "real" returns) highlight the unrelenting impact of inflation on an investor's purchasing power.

Table 2.1 Comparison Of Nominal And Real Returns For Stocks And Bonds Over Various Periods (1930-1998)

Investment types /inflation	Long-term returns 1930-98		Post-war returns 1946-98		Rapid-inflation 1970-79		Disinflation returns 1980-89	
	Nominal	Inflation-adjusted	Nominal	Inflation-adjusted	Nominal	Inflation-adjusted	Nominal	Inflation-adjusted
S&P 500-stock Index	10.40%	7.08%	12.30%	7.77%	5.40%	-1.86%	17.30%	11.61%
Long-term government bonds	5%	1.80%	5.20%	0.96%	5.50%	-1.77%	12.60%	7.14%
Inflation rate	3.10%		4.20%		7.40%		5.10%	

Some interesting conclusions can be drawn from the table. The first message is long-term bonds may let you sleep well at night but at a price—in this case lost performance. Next, in all cases presented, returns from stocks outperform the returns from bonds, except during rapid-inflationary times. During expanding inflationary periods, returns of both stocks and bonds drop, and *both underperform the inflation rate*. Therefore the inflation-adjusted values for the S&P 500 and long-term government bonds are negative numbers.

Just the opposite happens during disinflationary times. Both bonds and stocks prosper during disinflationary periods, as experienced by the inflation-adjusted results of the decade of the eighties. Finally, the disinflationary rates of the nineties (not shown) are driving returns back toward the mean of the last 70 years—the long-term inflation rate is 3% while nominal and inflation-adjusted returns of stock are in high double-digits.

Stocks Are The Long-Term Winners.

Historically, stocks have kept investors far ahead of bonds, money market investments, or inflation. Why? The potential riskiness of the stock market in the short run is the corollary to why, in the long run, the market is the best place to invest. Companies sell stock when they need to raise capital but are unsure of the returns their investments will generate. To persuade investors to buy, companies must offer a promise of reward substantially greater than the rewards those investors could achieve by holding bonds or money market securities. In diversified portfolios, such as the 500 companies of the S&P 500, stock investments that succeed have more than compensated for those that have failed.

If an investor bought $1,000 of long-term government bonds in 1930 and reinvested all of the interest, at the end of 1998, such an investment would have accumulated a risk-adjusted value of just over $1,855. If an investor bought the S&P 500 for $1,000 in 1930 and reinvested all dividends, at the end of 1998, the risk-adjusted investment would be worth nearly $153,000. That's a dramatic difference. And, an investor can expect to do even better than this example if investments are managed wisely—for example, by using the Y-Process investment strategy presented in Part Three of this book.

The Risk Of Risk-Free Bonds.

Buying a bond fund to hold indefinitely is a high-risk approach that an intelligent investor would never consider. The only higher risk approach is to invest your money *only* in bonds. Investors in the millions thought they were making a safe decision investing in long-term bond funds in the past. Many of them lost money.

However, bonds belong in your investment plan for good reasons, but possibly not for the reasons most investors think. Some examples:

Economic forces that depress stock prices in the early stages of a recession tend to boost bond prices.

Bonds can generate impressive profits from capital gains. How? When the original bonds are bought at a discount and suddenly the prime rate is reduced significantly. This results in an immediate jump in the value of the bond.

Bonds can provide a predictable stream of relatively high income that you can use for living expenses or for funding other parts of your investment plan.

Certain types of bonds offer valuable tax advantages and unique opportunities to invest a modest amount with a reasonable prospect of collecting a large amount years later.

Note that the word "safety" does not appear on the list. Many investors think bonds are among the safest investments, but such a notion can be costly. Bonds entail several kinds of risks, each of which will be covered in this chapter

What You Need To Know About Bonds. Bonds are IOUs issued by corporations, state and city governments and their agencies, and the federal government and its agencies. When you buy a bond, you become a creditor of the corporation or agency; it owes you the amount shown on the face of the bond, plus interest. You get a fixed amount of interest on a regular schedule—every six months in most cases—until the bond matures after a specified number of years, at which time you are paid the bond's face value. If the issuer goes broke, bondholders have first claim, ahead of stockholders.

Balancing Risk And Rewards. Many seasoned investors in the decade of the nineties, in the years where double-digit gains in the stock market were commonplace, may have been seduced into putting all their cash into stocks. For these people and many others, the current dilemma is whether to stay invested in the market or boost their fixed-income holdings. Just what investment mix makes sense is a matter of sharp debate, even among investment professionals.

Investment authorities insist that you should always have fixed-income assets (bonds) in your portfolio for funds that are needed in the next several years. Many pension funds, for instance, have traditionally balanced risk and return with a mix of 60% stocks and 40% bonds.

The Relationship Between Price And Yield. When a new bond is issued, the interest rate it pays is called the *coupon rate*, which is the fixed annual payment expressed as a percentage of the face value. An 8% coupon bond pays $80 a year interest on each $1,000 of face value, a 9% coupon bond pays $90 and so on. That is what the issuer will pay—no more, no less— for the life of the bond. But it may or may not be the yield you can earn from that issue; understanding why is the key to unlocking the real potential of investing in bonds.

Take a bond offering with a coupon interest rate of 9%, meaning that it pays $90 a year for every $1,000 of face value. What happens if interest rates rise to 10% after the bond is issued? New bonds will have to pay a 10% coupon rate or no one will buy them. By the same token, you could sell your 9% bond only if you offered it at a price that produced a 10% yield for the buyer. So the price at which you could sell would be whatever $90 represents 10% of, which is $900. Thus, you lose $100 if you sell. Even if you do not sell, you suffer a paper loss because your bond is now worth $100 less than you paid for it. It is selling at a *discount*.

But what if interest rates were to decline? Say rates drop to 8% while you are holding your 9% bond. New bonds would be paying only 8% and you could sell your old bond for the value of what $90 represents 8% of. Because $90 is 8% of $1,125, selling your 9% bond when interest rates are at 8% would produce a $125 capital gain. That $125 is called a *premium*. Actual prices are also affected by the time remaining before the bond matures and by the likelihood of the issue being "called," that is, when a company elects to redeem the bond prior to its maturity date.

The Risks Of Bonds. Interest rate changes create one of the chief risks you face as an investor in bonds. The single most important thing to remember about the relationship between the market value of the bonds you hold and changes in current interest rates: *As interest rates rise, bond prices fall; as interest rates fall, bond prices rise. The further away the bond's maturity or call date, the more volatile its price tends to be.*

Interest rate rises are not the only potential risk for bond investors. Another risk is the chance that the organization that issued the bonds won't be able to pay them off. Assessing the credit worthiness of companies and government agencies issuing bonds is a job for the pros. The best known is Standard & Poors and Moody. Standard and Poors assigns investment grades to the companies from AAA, AA, A or BBB. For these grades the risk of default is low. Grades below BBB are considered either "speculative" (BB or B) or in real danger of default (various levels of C and a D indicate that the issue is close to or actually in default). You can consider any issue rated speculative or lower to be a "junk" bond, although brokers and mutual funds usually call them "high-yield" issues.

Treasuries: The Safest Bonds Of All. One way to eliminate the default risk entirely is to stick with IOUs from the U.S. Treasury. Because the federal government backs them, there is virtually no chance that you will miss getting a payment of interest or principal or that Uncle Sam's credit rating will be lowered. Buying Treasuries does not eliminate the market risk, however; once issued, their value fluctuates with interest rates, just like corporate bonds. But the risk of default is nil.

Treasuries have other attractive features as well. Interest (but not capital gains) is exempt from state and local income taxes. Because the market for them is so vast, they are easy to buy and easy to sell. Commissions tend to be modest. In fact, you can buy Treasuries direct at regularly scheduled auctions (you do not have to attend) and eliminate commission charges entirely.

All these advantages do come at a price though. Treasuries tend to yield a little less than corporate bonds with comparable maturity, even AAA-rated corporate. But for the peace of mind they provide, that is a small price to pay. Table 2.2 provides a brief overview of the characteristics of the five most prominent types of bonds. This overview of the world of bonds is a handy reference for the future.

Risk-Reducing Steps That You Should Take As A Bond Investor. Bond
investors should consider certain aspects of the purchase prior to the purchase, such as, the ideal time to buy, potential volatility, diversification-using maturity dates, safety ratings and types of bonds. The set of rules listed below will serve as a handy reference for bond buyers.

• **Do not buy bonds when interest rates are low or rising.** Put your cash in a money-market fund or in certificates of deposit maturing in three to nine months. The ideal time to buy bonds is when interest rates have stabilized at a relatively high level or when they seem about to head down.

• **Reduce the potential volatility of your bond holdings.** Stick to short- and intermediate-term issues with maturities of three to five years. They fluctuate less in price than longer-term issues and they don't require you to tie up your money for 10 or more years in exchange for a relatively small additional yield.

Table 2.2 Classes And Characteristics Of Bonds

Type of Bond	Par Value	Maturity Period	Trading Details	Rated	Tax Status	Call Provisions[6]
Corporate Bonds[1]	$1K	Short Term:1-5 yrs. Intermediate:5-10 yrs.	By brokers on any exchange or OTC	Yes	Taxable	Callable
Municipal Bonds[2]	$5K and up	From 1 mo. to 40 yrs.	By brokers or OTC; often, investment bankers underwrite whole issues and resell to dealers and brokers.	Yes	Exempt from federal taxes. Exempt from state and local taxes under special conditions	Sometimes callable
T-Bonds and T-Notes[3]	$1K, $5K, $10K, $100K, and $1M	Bonds—over 10 yrs. Notes—2-10 yrs.	New issues: by auction at any Federal Reserve Bank. Outstanding issues: by brokers or OTC.	Not rated. Risk-free	Exempt from state and local taxes	Usually not callable
T-Bills[4]	$10K (also issued in amounts up to $1M)	3 months, 6 months, 1 year.	New issues: by auction at any FRB Outstanding issues: by brokers or OTC	Not rated. Risk-free	Exempt from state and local taxes	Not callable
Agency Bonds[5], e.g., bonds of mortgage associations; Ginnie Mae, Fannie Mae and Freddie Mac.	$1K to $25K and higher.	30 days to 20 yrs.	By brokers or OTC; directly through banks	Some issues are rated by some services	Taxable, but federal agency bonds are exempt from state and local taxes.	Not callable

1. These bonds are readily available to investors as companies use them rather than bank loans to finance expansion and other activities.

2. More than ones million municipal bonds have been issued by states, cities, and other local governments to pay for construction and other projects.

3. These long-term debt issues of the Federal government are a major source of government funding to keep operations running and to pay interest on the national debt.

4. Treasury bills are the largest component of the money market—the market for short-term debt securities. The government uses them to raise money for immediate spending at lower rates than bonds or notes.

5. Federal and state agencies also issue bonds to raise money for their operations and projects.

6. A call provision is an option, written into the security's provisions, whereby the issuer may redeem the bond prior to its maturity date.

• **Diversify your bond holdings by acquiring bonds with different maturity dates.** A mix of issues maturing in one, three and five years will protect you from getting hurt by interest rate movements you can not control. (Mutual funds, which are discussed in the next chapter, are an excellent way to achieve diversity in your bond investments.)

• **Do not buy any bond with a safety rating lower than A.** Watch for news that may affect the rating while you own the bond.

• **Invest for maximum safety of principal.** Stick with bonds issued by the U.S. Treasury Department.

3

Mutual Funds—
The Ideal Investment For Beginners

START WITH JUST ONE NO-LOAD INDEX FUND IF THAT'S ALL YOU CAN AFFORD

Mutual Funds And What They Have To Offer. Mutual funds are among the most flexible and potentially advantageous investments. They are especially suited for the beginning investor. The mutual fund industry has grown almost exponentially since the first fund was formed in 1924. At this writing there are over 8,000 funds (more than there is stock on the New York Stock Exchange) investing greater than $4 trillion on behalf of stockholders. Some funds have no minimum investment requirement. You can buy $25 worth of shares if you want. A typical minimum is $1,000 to open an account, with minimum additional investments of $50 or $100. This makes mutual funds ideal vehicles for long-term accumulation programs thorough dollar-cost averaging.

Funds come in various types, sizes, and shapes, with different strategies and objectives. This chapter focuses in on just two types of funds *1) Money Market Funds* and *2) Index Funds*. For the novice investor, it will take a year or so of investing and following your funds in the financial

51

section of your local newspaper before you're ready to move on to the next level of investing.

Before we get into the specifics, an overview of the concepts, advantages and limitations of mutual funds is in order. A mutual fund is simply an investment company that sells shares of its stock to the public, and invests the proceeds in an investment mix of stocks and bonds of other companies. Mutual fund stockholders share in the income, profits, and losses of their funds' investments. At the end of every business day, the typical fund calculates the total market value of all of its investments and deducts its liabilities to determine the value of each outstanding share.

• **Automatic diversification.** The single greatest advantage of a mutual fund is that it is *a portfolio* of many securities. Owning shares of a mutual fund gives you a small ownership interest in all the stocks, bonds and other investments in the fund's portfolio. Whether your aim is to own a cross section of growth stocks or high-tech stocks you can find a fund or funds to suit you. Because they provide instant diversification, well-selected mutual funds are a better choice than individual stocks (or bonds) for investors with modest amounts of money to place at risk.

• **A family of funds.** Most mutual fund companies offer investors a family of individual funds. A family may include stock, bond, and money funds, international stock and bond funds. The company's managers pride themselves on offering many types of individual funds and hire experts who make the investment decisions for each fund. Because they provide expert portfolio management, investing in a fund is a better choice than investing in a portfolio of individual stocks, especially for beginning investors who are still unsure of their own stock-picking prowess.

• **Mutual funds provide selection flexibility.** Investors may find it convenient to invest only in a single mutual fund's family, using the company's resources as their core account and broker. But most of the major investment companies act as a one-stop resource for investing in other popular mutual fund companies. A toll-free call is all it takes to buy, sell, or exchange shares in thousands of different funds. For example, *Fidelity Investments*, the largest mutual fund Company in the world, has close to 200 individual mutual funds in its family. Some investors may want to add other choices, from other fund families, into their portfolio.

• **Ease of purchase and sale.** You can buy funds through a broker or through the mail. You can sell them the same way or with an 800-number phone call. By law, a fund must buy back its shares when you want to sell them. The price at which fund shares are bought and sold is based on the fund's *net asset value*, which is the market value of the fund's holdings, minus management expenses, divided by the number of shares outstanding. The price you pay or receive will be based on the net asset value calculated at the close of trading on the day you place your order. Many mutual funds impose a "sales charge" or "load" on investors that buy new shares. A major difference between "load" and "no-load" funds is that you buy and sell no-load funds at their net asset value plus a commission, but sell them back to the fund at their net asset value. Later in this chapter I cover the many types of mutual fund costs.

• **Small minimums and fractional purchases.** Some funds have no minimum investment requirements. You can buy $25 worth if you want. More typically, funds have a minimum of $1,000 to open an account, with minimum additional investments of $50 or $100. As noted earlier, this makes funds ideal vehicles for long-term accumulation programs through dollar cost averaging.

One nice advantage of funds is that their price per share doesn't affect how much you can invest, since funds sell fractional shares, which is not done with normal stock purchases. So if you want to invest $1,000 and the fund is $17.56 a share, you get 56.948 shares. If the price is $2.96 a share, you get 338 shares. Also, the price per share of a fund should never be a consideration in your investment decision. A $4 a share fund can increase or drop in percentage just as far a percentage and as fast as a $400 share fund.

• **Automatic reinvestment of earnings.** You can request that dividends paid by stocks in the fund's portfolio and the interest from bonds and capital gains earned from selling securities be reinvested automatically in more shares. Reinvested earnings is a critical element in any long-term investment plan.

• **Automatic payment plans.** If you would like to receive regular income from your shares, funds will set up automatic payment plans for you. If dividends and interest earned aren't enough to cover the payments to you, the fund will sell shares to cover them.

• **Shareholder services.** Most funds have set up well-staffed telephone systems to handle inquiries about everything from current account balances to requests for descriptive brochures and order forms. Funds love individual retirement accounts or 401K accounts because they know such accounts are likely to stay there for some years. Funds have simplified the custodial paperwork to the point that it is virtually painless for the investor.

Another advantage about owning funds is that they do most of the paperwork for their stockholders. Capital gains and losses on the purchase and sale of securities, as well as dividend and interest earnings, are neatly totaled for each stockholder at the end of the year for their tax purposes. Funds also do all of the day-to-day paperwork chores, including handling of stock certificates, brokerage tickets, statements, transfer agents, etc. All an investor has to do is send their money to a fund and it does the rest.

• **Moving money.** Another advantage of a mutual fund family is the ease to switch your money from one member of the family to another, usually with a phone call. That provides a convenient way for you to move your money from, say, a stock fund to a money-market fund.

Mutual Fund Costs—Loads, Fees, And Expenses. Investing in mutual funds may be the road to riches but there's no free lunch. Investors owning a

stock mutual fund subject themselves to a variety of costs, fees and charges as well as taxes on any profit and capital gains.

• **Sales charges.** Many mutual funds impose a "sales charge" or "load" on investors that buy new shares. Suppose that the load published by a fund is 8.5 percent. Suppose the fund has a 10 percent total return the first year you own it. What is the sales fee and what is the return? A load of 8.5 percent means that $850 of a $10,000 investment is kept by the broker, so only $9,150 of your money was placed in the fund. The sales fee equals 9.3 percent* of the amount actually invested by you but you still earned 10 percent on the amount invested, or $915, not 10% on $10,000. Sadly, most funds quote their sales charges as a percentage of the cost of shares purchased plus the commission. Such a deceptive practice makes commission rates appear to be slightly lower than they really are.

Taking fees into account is important when calculating your gain, but in comparing funds, keep in mind that a fund's total return is a fund's total return, period. A sales fee, if any, doesn't mean that the return on your investment is lower, it means that less of your money is invested initially. Sales charges are usually reduced for larger transactions.

Many mutual funds, including virtually all money market mutual funds, are "no-load" and do not charge any sales loads at all. I recommend that using a check cashing capability use money market funds as a "holding account" where you can draw money out of the fund.

• **Redemption fee.** When an investor sells (redeems) shares back to the fund, they may incur another charge, a redemption fee. Most funds do not have redemption fees, but some charge up to 5.3 percent of the amount of money initially invested. "Back-end loads," are sales charges deducted at the end of the transaction rather than the beginning. However, the charges usually scale down with the passing of time. For example, a fund might charge a five percent redemption fee on the sale of

---

* 9.3%=($850 divided by $915) times 100

shares sold within one year of purchase, while shares sold in their second year would incur a four percent fee, and so on down to a one percent fee in the fifth year, and nothing thereafter.

Other funds levy a small redemption fee on the full sale value of shares sold within a specified period—say, within the first six months or one-year after purchase. Such redemption fees are usually imposed to discourage investors from frequent trading.

• **Reinvestment fees.** Nearly all funds permit investors to automatically reinvest all capital gains and income distributions in new shares with no sales charge.

• **Rule 12b-1 Fees.** When you buy a fund from a broker, you pay a sales charge or commission, typically for the advice they offer. Commissions have been around as long as mutual funds. But in 1980, the Securities and Exchange Commission (SEC) wrote Rule 12b-1, authorizing fund companies to add a new annual charge for marketing and distribution, which might include advertising costs or an annual payout to the broker who sold you the fund. Fee's, and other fund expenses, are deducted each and every year from the fund's assets.

In July 1992, the National Association of Securities Dealers capped the 12b-1 at .75 percent to recover the sales commission but then added another .25 percent as a broker's service fee. They are nothing more than a different type of hidden load. Whether such charges are said to be pursuant to a distribution plan or an administration services agreement, they end up enriching salesmen and fund sponsors, not investors.

How To Address Mutual Fund Costs. It is evident, that fund investors should avoid sales charges, redemption fees, hidden loads, and service fees. Be an informed investor and be aware of all costs of fund ownership.

The message is clear. If you must buy a load fund, or one that charges a commission, get one with a front-end load and no 12b-1 fee. You're better off with a straightforward, up-front haircut on your investment than little nibbles over the years. Note: Most investors would incur far lower costs themselves if they bypassed mutual funds and purchased "index stock" directly. We'll cover this topic in Part Two. There are other costs (on both load and no-load funds) to know about: (These costs are collected by the fund sponsors by lowering the value of the stock when it is calculated on a daily basis.)

• **Transaction costs.** As a fund buys and sells securities, it incurs brokerage commissions. Transaction costs are normally much lower for mutual funds than for individual investors because funds buy and sell in large quantities. Nevertheless, all trading costs are ultimately borne by shareholders. The more actively a fund turns over (trades) its portfolio, naturally, the more transaction costs it will incur.

• **Portfolio management fees.** Every mutual fund contracts with an investment advisor to make investment decisions. Shareholders must bear the cost of the fee paid to the manager, which usually ranges from 0.25 percent to 1 1/4 percent of fund assets per annum. Generally, the larger the fund, the lower the percentage fee. Annual management fees in excess of 0.75 percent should generally be considered excessive.

• **Operating expenses.** Mutual funds incur various day-to-day operating costs, including rent, telephone expense, employee salaries, prospectus and annual report printing, and so forth. As these expenses are incurred, they are paid from fund assets, and therefore reduce stockholders' returns. Typical fund operating expenses range from 0.10 percent to 1 1/4 percent per year. Added to management fees, total operating expenses exceed 2 percent per annum for some funds. Total annual expenses average 1.45 percent for all equity funds, 1.05 percent for all taxable bond funds, and 0.85 percent for all tax-free bond funds.

Load Vs. No-Load Funds. There are two primary reasons to choose a load fund: you need investment advice or you've located a special money manager who is available only in a load fund.

If you have an interest in investing in funds, there are many sources available to help in selecting your own funds. There is much information available from *Morningstar Mutual Funds*, a Chicago Ill mutual fund analysis firm, which started operations in 1984. The availability of information and heightened consumer interest has shifted the balance from broker-sold funds toward funds that are sold direct to the investor. Fidelity is a good example of the blurring of the line between load and no-load groups. It sells funds a number of ways: directly to the public without a sales charge, directly to the public with a sales charge, through registered representatives, and through its own fee-based advisory service.

• **Do you get what you pay for?** The notion that you "get what you pay for" does not apply to mutual funds. There is no assurance that funds with loads have anything extra to offer an investor. Numerous studies bolster that insight. One study by Morningstar proves the point. Morningstar divided its mutual fund universe into two groups in mid-1995 to study the difference between load and no-load funds. It found that load funds had a higher annual expense ratio—1.62 percent, on average, compared with 1.11 percent for no-load funds. It also found that no-load funds are a bit less aggressive, on average, in investment style. As for performance, the no-load funds outperformed in the short run when the load-fund performance was adjusted to account for loads.

Another 23-year performance study by the *Buyer's Guide* of no-load funds provides definitive proof that no-load funds reward their shareholders with superior returns. And that superiority exists *before* adjusting for sales charges. In other words, the performance gap widens further in favor of no-load funds when sales loads are charged against the performance of the load funds. Put another way, sales charges do not buy superior performance, they just buy a salesman.

Table 3.1 Growth Funds Annual Rates of Return: 1971-1993

Years	No-Load Funds Only	All Funds (Load and No-Load)
1971-1975	-0.40%	-1.00%
1976-1980	24.00%	16.90%
1981-1985	11.20%	11.20%
1986-1990	10.50%	10.20%
1991-1993	23.10%	21.10%
All 23 Years	12.50%	10.60%

Table 3.1 displays the performance of all U.S. growth funds over five separate intervals from 1971 through 1993. "All growth funds" in the table included both load and no-load growth funds. In each period shown, *no-load* funds performed as well, or better, than *all funds* combined. Over the entire 23 years, no-loads provided an average annual return of 12.5%, the equivalent of an initial $10,000 investment growing to $150,000. Meanwhile all growth funds returned only 10.6% per year, the equivalent of an initial $10,000 investment increasing to $101,400.

What is the fund's expense ratio? The expense ratio shows how the costs of running the fund eat up much of your potential earnings. The fund must deduct expenses (except for sales fees) before calculating its total return, and hence the total return is a much more important number. On the other hand, if you're going to invest in an "index fund" that invests in a stock market index, e.g., the DJIA or the S&P 500, pay close attention to its expense ratio. Since an index fund is designed to track an actual stock index, a high expense ratio will tend to load the fund down and drop its return below the actual stock index's return.

Advantages And Limitations Of Money Market Funds. The standard of excellence in the consumer money market is a well-run money market mutual fund (money fund, for short). Nearly every mutual fund family and every stockbroker offers a money fund. Money funds have been around since 1970 and have an unblemished track record for safety, liquidity, and competitive yields. The earnings on their portfolios determine their returns. Perhaps the best part of the deal is that managers obtain high yields while taking only 0.47 percent, on average, of the funds' assets per year in management fees.

They offer the best combination of safety, liquidity and yield. And if you are in a mutual fund family, when you sell a stock fund the assets can be moved into a safe haven money fund.

• **Money funds are not insured.** *Money funds* are not insured as are bank or fund *money market* deposit accounts, but no money fund has ever failed or is ever likely to fail. So why give up 1 percent or more in interest to invest in a bank money market account?

• **Unlimited free checking privileges.** As an extra-added attraction, money funds offer benefits that *bank* money market deposit accounts do not. Many offer unlimited free checking privileges, and most offer free wiring of money to a bank account, and convenient access to other investments in a mutual fund family. There is one limitation that may be considered a drawback; most money funds require that a minimum check value of $500 be written.

• **Primary money fund limitation.** You do not know exactly how much you will earn. But, if interest rates are rising you will probably earn more than a bank CD would offer, and if they are falling, you will be elsewhere making a killing in your stock fund.

• **Tax-free money market funds.** Tax-free money market funds are an exciting development of the 1980s. These funds operate much like taxable money market funds, but they invest in short-term money market instruments issued by municipalities, state governments, and government authorities. The interest payments are exempt from federal income tax.

You can decide whether a tax-free money market fund makes sense for you by converting a tax-free money fund's yield to its "taxable equivalent." You do this by multiplying the tax-free fund's yield by a factor derived from your tax bracket and then you can compare it with a taxable alternative. For instance, if you are in the 28 percent federal tax bracket and the investment you are considering is not exempt from your state's taxes, the conversion multiplier is 1.389. If you are in the 31 percent federal tax bracket, the conversion multiplier is 1.449. To determine these conversion multipliers divide one by your appropriate tax bracket either 1.28 or 1.31.

In several states with high state income taxes, such as New York, California, and Massachusetts, double tax-free money funds have been offered. These funds invest in in-state tax-exempt instruments, so their income is exempt from state taxes as well. Triple tax-free money funds are available to New York City residents. These invest in New York City tax-exempt issues and are triple exempt from state, local, and federal taxes.

• **Money fund credit risk.** Credit risk should never be an issue in the money market. The money market is a very exclusive club. Consumers should always deal exclusively with risk-free (federally guaranteed) or regulated money market institutions. Securities and Exchange Commission (SEC) mutual fund regulations make mutual funds essentially as safe as banks. All investments by money funds must be kept in a bank trust department. No money fund manager has access to the investments, so no one can run off to an offshore island with the money. The SEC also regulates money funds' investment practices. No money fund has ever invested in anything that did not pay off as agreed at maturity.

Index Funds: Buying The "Benchmark." Most investments promise to beat the averages, to help you do better than the next guy. Indexing uses

a very different approach. An index fund simply buys a large number (or all) of the securities listed in an index—seeking to duplicate that index's performance. The first index ever developed was by The Vanguard Group. Vanguard developed the *500 Portfolio* that seeks to track the performance of the S&P 500 composite-stock index, which emphasizes stocks of large U.S. companies. By its nature, indexing emphasizes broad diversification, minimal trading activity, and razor-thin costs. As a result, index investors benefit from a reduction of certain investment risks, the possibility of lower taxable distributions, and the ability to keep a higher percentage of investment returns.

Back in 1975, when the Vanguard Group, started developing its first index fund, indexing was in its infancy. Paul Samuelson, the Nobel laureate economist, started a lively intellectual debate about what he saw as the obvious advantages of indexing. Samuelson argued that although all stock pickers and mutual fund managers try to beat the market average, few succeed. In fact, on average, it has been determined that the performance of 75 percent of all mutual funds lag behind the market average every year.

There are good reasons for mutual funds to lag behind the S&P 500 index. The costs of trading, administration, and other fees mean that fund managers must beat the market index by about 2 percent, if they are to come out even after expenses. For example, Vanguard has done a good job of tracking the average. From August 1976 through August 1987, the fund earned a 407.7 percent rate of return, compared to 435.0 percent for the S&P 500 composite-stock index.

• **Indexing reduces investor cost.** A traditional mutual fund buys and sells securities based on the fund manager's judgments about which stocks are likely to provide the greatest return to investors. This traditional "active" approach typically gives fund managers latitude in managing the fund's holdings. As a result, investors in these funds are often not entirely sure how their money is being invested at a given moment. Also, the fund's performance, which is dependent on the adviser's strategies and tactics, comes at a significant yearly cost: typically 1% to 2% or more of assets invested.

Indexing's "passive" approach is more objective and predictable, and available for as little as one-sixth the yearly cost. As its name implies, index investing relies on indexes that combine groups of stocks to measure the performance of the total market or a specific market segment.

The idea behind indexing was to minimize trading, eliminate management fees, and reduce the other costs of doing business by simply putting together a basket of the same stocks that make up the total market index. An investor who bought into this mutual fund would get performance that matched the market at a very low cost. Institutional investors loved this idea of reducing costs and risk.

The concept caught on more slowly with individual investors, although the Vanguard fund did its job of tracking the market and cutting expenses. When Vanguard brought out the fund, the expense ratio was 45 basis points, (0.45 percent) of assets under management. By 1988, it had dropped to 26 basis points followed by another drop in 1997 to 19 basis points. That compares to an average equity fund expense ratio of 110 basis points or 1.1 percent. To put it another way, on an investment of $10,000, the annual management fee would be $19 for the Vanguard fund compared to $110 for the average stock fund. In 1986, Vanguard took the idea of indexing one step further. It introduced the Extended Market Portfolio, which buys stocks in the Wilshire 4500 index (a broadly diversified index of stocks of medium-size and small U.S. companies). This is an index of all stocks traded, except for the S&P 500. Now an investor can buy the entire market by putting together a combination of the two indexes. Bogle, the CEO of Vanguard, said "We think we'll move from the idea of index matching to market matching, If you buy 70 percent of the S&P and 30 percent of the Extended Market Portfolio, then you'll match the overall market."

• **Buy the market.** The goal of an index fund is to track the performance of the stock market. When the total market advances, a good index fund follows. When the market declines, so does the fund. The fund gets its name because it follows a broad index of the market. Rather than using a portfolio manager to pick stocks that he/she thinks will outperform the market, an index fund uses investors' money to purchase a group of stocks that are weighted in the same way as a broad market index. For example, a typical stock index fund contains the same stocks as the Standard & Poors 500 stock index, a broad gauge of the market. Table 3.2 provides a partial list of the mutual fund industry that tracks the S&P 500 index funds.

• **Passive management.** An index fund holds roughly the same securities in the same relative amounts all the time, so there's no need for a manager. Instead, these funds are "passively managed. "That simply means that the securities are bought and held. They are rarely traded. Some active mutual fund managers move out of the market and into cash when they think the market is weak. But an index fund is always fully invested in the securities of the index it tracks.

• **An index fund offers advantages and disadvantages.** Obviously, you are better off simply "owning the market" with an index fund than investing in a mutual fund that underperforms the market. An index fund will *never* outperform the market, but neither should it underperform by much. A good index fund will closely track the movement of the index it follows, falling slightly shy of the market's performance because of administrative fees. Secondly, because index funds are not actively managed or traded, there isn't a management fee. Finally, an index fund saves you from the chore of picking a money manager and monitoring his performance. If you believe that the stock market is a good bet over time but you don't want to bother with these details, an index fund is a good choice for you.

• **Institutional investors love indexing.** The really influential investors are the institutional investors who invest billions of dollars for pension funds, insurance companies, and mutual funds. Because they invest in such large quantities, they pay less in fees, commissions, and expenses than individual investors do. This resembles the wholesale and retail business in any product area. For example, a restaurateur buys his meat in the wholesale market, where he pays far less per pound for a porterhouse steak, because of the quantity he buys, than you pay in the retail market when you visit your local butcher.

Because of their low cost and their ability to track the market, index funds have long appealed to institutional investors. Costs to these big-money managers are extremely low, much less than an individual investor pays. For example, a typical fee for an actively managed institutional fund is 40 basis points. But for an index fund, that fee is 8 basis points, or .08 percent of assets under management.

Individual investors must pay more for index funds than institutions do (see Table 3.2). And many mutual fund companies have been reluctant to offer them to the public at all.

Even if you're a conservative investor, an index fund can work for a portion of your money. Your investment is almost certain to grow much more quickly than it would in any guaranteed bank account. Your biggest risk is that you might need the money at a time when the market is in the doldrums. For that reason, it's always prudent to put only a part of your portfolio in stocks. If you want to buy an index fund, first check the performance of the index that the fund purports to mimic. Next, check to see how close the fund has come to tracking the index, also check the expense ratio. As you can see in Table 3.2, the expense ratio can vary from 15 to 133 basis points. A true index fund should have low costs and it should demonstrate good success in following the index.

Table 3.2 Partial List Of Index Funds That Track The S&P 500 Composite-Stock Index (June 1999)

Fund Name	Expense ratio	Fund Name	Expense ratio
Aon S&P 500	.29 %	Munder Index 500 A	.39 %
BT Index Funds 500	.25 %	One Group Eq Index A	.60 %
BullPro Fund	1.33 %	Schwab S&P 500	.35 %
California Inv Tr S&P500	.20 %	Schwab S&P 500 Select	.19 %
DFA U.S. Large	.15 %	Scudder S&P 500	.40 %
Dreyfus BASIC S&P 500	.20 %	SEI S&P 500 A	.25 %
Dreyfus S&P 500	.50 %	SSgA S&P 500	.17 %
Fidelity Spartan Market	.19 %	Strong Index 500	.45 %
First American Eq Index	.60 %	T. Rowe Price Equity Idx	.40 %
Galaxy II Large Co.	.40 %	Transamerica Premier	.25 %
INVESCO S&P 500 I	.55 %	USAA S&P 500 Index	.18 %
Kent Index Equity	.68 %	Vanguard Index 500	.19 %
Northern Funds Stock Ind	.55 %	Victory Stock Index	.57 %

PART TWO

ASSISTING THE INTERMEDIATE INVESTOR TO BECOME A MORE EFFECTIVE MANAGER AT BUILDING WEALTH

(Chapters 4 through 6)

Preface: Part Two is written for the intermediate investor. A majority of intermediate investors are long-term; buy-and-hold investors with diversified portfolios pursuing their journey of wealth building to support a comfortable retirement. The objective of this part is to help the informed, risk-sensitive intermediate-investor to become a more effective manager of their portfolio, with renewed confidence in making risk-reward decisions. After you complete this part, you will be prepared to go on to part three and learn about more sophisticated investment strategies. You will learn about a unique active management strategy that instructs the investor on how to assess risk and make trading decisions using the "Y-Process." This part of the book also teaches the investor how to use the Y-Process to preserve capital during market downturns and reenter the market—after the worst is over-to enhance total returns.

4

The Psychology
Of Investing

WE ALL SUCCUMB TO ANY NUMBER OF HUMAN FAILINGS THAT COST US THOUSANDS OF DOLLARS EACH YEAR. LEARN TO SORT OUT THE PSYCHOLOGICAL FACTORS THAT AFFECT YOUR INVESTMENT DECISIONS.

Mistakes In Investing Decisions. Even today, after the 1990s decade of stunning gains in the stock market, there are investors who just hate themselves, full of remorse over their bad investment decisions and missed opportunities. In fact, that characterization probably describes most investors, since even small failures seem to stand out more than the successes. Despite all our emphasis on hard, cold, clear-headed analysis, emotion often governs investing decisions. People make financial mistakes for many reasons. No matter how smart we think we are, we all make mistakes about money that cost us thousands of dollars every year—often without being aware of them. The culprits: a series of mental blind spots and knee-jerk reactions that befog financial judgments. We listen to poor advice. We succumb to euphoria, fear, anxiety, over-confidence and any number of other human failures.

This chapter is not about the stock in trade of self-appointed experts who blather on about the "psychology of money making", and charge high fees for all too-obvious advice. Rather, it focuses on more common and insidious mental errors that just about every investor makes often, partly because investors aren't aware of them. These mistakes are inbred; they are the universal byproduct of the shortcuts that are built into our machinery to enable us to cope with the intricacies of life.

Researchers have spent years sorting out the psychological factors that affect us when we enter the stock market. "They are like optical illusions," says psychologist Amos Tversky of Stanford, who, along with Daniel Kahneman of Berkeley, helped pioneer a study nearly three decades ago on fallacies in decision making. "Fortunately we can learn to recognize and compensate for many of the most common errors." Understanding how urges work can help investors keep damaging emotions under control.

Mistake Number One: Over-Confidence. Most of us have bountiful optimism and abundant self-confidence. In many ways, this is a useful trait. Self-confident, optimistic people tend to be happier, more motivated and more likely to persevere. But when we turn these characteristics to investing, optimism and self-confidence can become our downfall. Innate over-confidence makes us too quick to assume that what we know is accurate and complete—particularly when our information is sketchy. In the financial world, you're not interacting with people; you're interacting with prices. Prices don't care how you feel that day. In general, over-confidence is a negative characteristic.

Studies suggest that investors err in fairly consistent ways. We react too much to short-term performance. We overestimate the chances of success with long-shot investments, like initial public offerings and risky technology stocks. We see patterns in stock market returns where there are none. We sell stock-market winners too quickly while hanging on to losers too long. Finally, the more you trade the more poor decisions you are likely to make. Then you pay further through trading cost and lost opportunities.

• **Advice for over-confidence:** To overcome this mental lapse, one investment adviser suggests writing down everything known that might affect the outcome for each investment and purchase. Next, list what you don't know that might be important. Ponder the lists, before making your decision. And take note, however long your list, of the things you don't know, the true list is probably much longer.

Mistake Number Two: Fear Of Loss. Research has shown that most investors are averse to risk, preferring a sure thing to an alternative that's less certain but potentially more profitable. Studies have shown that *people hate to lose a dollar more than they like to win a dollar.* Most people prefer not to take risks that could reduce their profits, even if the risk offers the chance of making more. But they will take big risks to try to avoid a loss, even if the risk may deepen their loss.

One study of this phenomenon asked people to choose between two alternatives:

1) Imagine that someone has just handed you $1000. Now you must choose between these two options:

   Option A: You win $500 more for sure.
   Option B: You take an even chance of doubling that $1000 or winning nothing more.

2) Imagine that someone has just handed your $2000. You must choose between the two options:

   Option A: You lose $500 for sure.
   Option B: You take an even chance of losing $1000 or losing nothing.

Tversky and Kahneman have found that in the first of these two situations, about 72 percent of the people choose option A—the sure gain. By contrast, in the second situation, only about 64 percent choose option A—the sure loss. That's odd, since the consequences are identical. In both situations, the sure thing—whether a gain or loss—leaves you with $1500. Likewise, each gamble offers an even chance of ending up with $1000 or $2000.

Why the inconsistent answers? Among other things, our willingness to take a risk depends upon how we view our current situation. *We tend to accept risk more readily when we see it as a chance to avoid a certain loss.* Therefore, we choose the second question's gamble to avoid the sure $500 loss. We are more conservative, however, when we consider opportunities to add to our financial gains; as a result, when we answer the first question, we take the sure $500 and refuse to gamble for the additional $1000.

• **Advice to alleviate fear of loss.** Not everyone has the stomach to be in the stock market. If you are susceptible to selling everything in a panic, you ought to avoid stocks and stock mutual funds.

There is always something to worry about. Avoid weekend thinking and ignore the latest dire predictions of newscasters. Nobody can predict interest rates, the future direction of the economy, or the stock market. Dismiss all such forecasts and concentrate on what's actually happening to the companies and mutual funds in which you've invested. Sell a stock because the company's fundamentals deteriorate, not because the sky is falling. Don't assume that past investment results are meaningful especially when you are considering short-term numbers.

When choosing a mutual fund for example, consider other factors, such as, how volatile it has been over the past one, three and five years. Look at the big picture—consider an individual investment as part of your total portfolio. And, most importantly, be sure you can afford to sustain the loss if the fund's value declines.

Mistake Number Three: Deep Regret Over Errors. Research has also shown that most people have a strong aversion to regret. Investors often try to avoid feelings of regret by holding on to poor investments when the logical and rational course of action is to unload them. Moreover, most people feel regret more deeply when it involves an *unwise action* that they have taken rather than when it is simply related to a *missed opportunity*.

One study of this phenomenon asked people what they would choose in the following two situations:

Situation A: You win $150 dinner with your spouse at a local restaurant next Saturday night. Then a friend invites the two of you, and another guest, to his home for dinner the same evening. The other guest is the candidate for Governor who you very much want to meet. Choose between the two dinners.

Situation B: You have paid $150 in advance to have dinner with your spouse (or significant other) at a local restaurant. The $150 is not refundable. Now you get the above invitation from your friend. Choose between the two dinners.

Most people find it hard to skip dinner at the restaurant in the second situation because they have already paid for it. But the $150 shouldn't affect their thinking since they can't get it back. Instead, they should decide which dinner would give them more pleasure and choose that one. *Future costs are what matter.* But often people can't forget the money they've spent in the past.

That pervasive problem offers a further explanation for our tendency to support lost causes. An example should reinforce this concept. Joseph Nestor, an engineer at General Electric, took a call from his stockbroker who persuaded him to invest $21,000 in HIP Reuters, a Health Maintenance Organization that trades on the American Stock Exchange. The stock fell from $10.50 to $2.50, but then Joseph shelled out another $7,500 for additional shares, hoping to recoup his loss. "The broker said it was a good idea." Joseph says. "I had to make up the difference some-how." Joseph continued to hold the shares, despite having absorbed a total loss of about $18,500 on his investment of $28,500.

• **Advice For Deep Regret Over Errors.** Don't look back and don't expect all of your decisions to be perfect. Generally, investors would make better decisions if they had no memory. Don't think about what you paid for a stock; instead consider whether *you would buy it at today's price.*

Mistake Number Four: We Frequently Overlook "Opportunity Cost." Researchers have found that most investors put an inflated value on things they own—a phenomenon known as the "endowment effect." As a result, they demand too high a price when they go to sell. By holding out, they often fail to sell when selling makes sense. The ideal selling opportunity may be missed; investors may lose the opportunity to move their money into something more profitable. This is called *opportunity cost.*

Take the case of Jack and Jill Jacoby. In 1997 they received an offer of $180,000 almost immediately after putting their Voorhees, NJ home on the market. But they turned it down because a friend who lived nearby had recently sold for $220,000. "Our home wasn't quite as nice as his," says Jack, a psychiatrist, "But we felt that if he had gotten $220,000 and we lived on the same block then we should hold out." Result? It took two years to find another buyer—at $145,000, or $35,000 less than the original offer.

The opportunity cost to Jack and Jill was not only the $35,000. They neglected to consider two additional costs. First, the two years of cost on the money they borrowed from a Savings and Loan Bank, at an 8.5 per-cent rate, for the new home they purchased, while their existing home was sitting there waiting for a buyer. The money they borrowed could have been reduced by the original offer of $180,000. Second, the two years of taxes they had to pay on their empty home while waiting for the sale to occur. These additional costs total $40,600. In all, the opportunity cost to Jack and Jill was $75,600.

Researchers have found that most people perceive continuous events in discrete or binary form—as up or down, black or white, successful or not. Therefore, they place special and even irrational importance on obtaining certain thresholds. Assume you bought a stock at 20. After two years it is still 20, and you decide it has little upside potential. Most people would sell. On the other hand, if the stock were 19 most investors infected with this "endowment effect" phenomenon would refuse to sell. Even if it meant leaving capital in an unpromising asset, they would hang on for years in the hope of "getting out even." Sound familiar?

• **Advice for frequently overlooked opportunity cost.** Before you spend, invest or turndown an offer to purchase your home, consider at least half a dozen other uses for the money. If you can do some fast—back of the envelope—calculations, determine the opportunity cost for rejecting a bid on your home or, for that matter, for hanging on to a poor performing mutual-fund or stock. When an investment performs poorly or is going nowhere, don't hang on too long if there is a potential for investing in some other asset that has a higher probability of enhancing your returns. On the other hand, if an investment posts gains, review the potential for additional profits before you decide to sell. The secret is to understand your own motives when you make a decision.

Mistake Number Five: Inability To Stick To An Investment Style And Strategy. Every trading session, the stock market offers its opinion. Ofttimes, investors are left scratching their heads, wondering whether they should listen. This is, of course, especially true when your stocks and stock-mutual-funds are getting clobbered. It's hard not to have doubts when you are losing money. When the broad stock market or a particular sector tumbles, some investors will extrapolate that short-term trend and expect prices to keep on falling. They're the ones who are most likely to jump. Other investors sit tight, but maybe not for long. Sticking with your strategy isn't always easy. The question is, how do you battle those doubts? Stick with your investment plan? Then when should you cave?

The keyword most Wall Street professionals use is *confidence*. *Buy-and-hold-and-pray* is a tough discipline. Certified Financial Planners advise that you should have a strong sense of where you're going (goals/objectives) and how you're going to get there (strategic plan). Often, that doesn't happen. Most people just get into the market and start mucking around.

There is a downside to confidence. The greater your expectations, the more likely you are to be disappointed. The skimpier your investment knowledge, the easier it is to get rattled. The more unfamiliar an investment, the greater the temptation to "cut and run" when the market declines. That's one good reason that it's so difficult for normal investors to invest in foreign stocks, and especially emerging markets. Whereas, it's relatively easy to own familiar investments like the Dow Jones blue-chip stocks. When circumstances are unfamiliar and values fall, we perceive high risk. *You have to manage your own expectations.* But, unswerving confidence should only extend so far. It can be helpful in fending off doubts about the amount that you have in stocks and the way that your investments are diversified. But when it comes to individual stocks and stock-mutual-funds, confidence shouldn't be confused with blind devotion, or marrying your stock "until death do you part."

• **Advice for sticking to your investment style and strategy.** Before you start dabbling in stocks and funds, go back to basics, i.e., settle on your asset allocation. Establish your target mix of stock mutual funds, bonds and cash investments, like Treasury-bills and money-market funds. Next, decide how to diversify your stock-market money among large-, medium- and small-capitalization funds. Thereafter, you shouldn't be swayed by the market's gyrations. This assumes your asset allocation and diversification make sense given your time horizon and stomach for risk.

As discussed in mistake number two—one reason people may stay with their investments is because they don't like to accept the loss. The danger for them comes when the market starts moving up again. As these investors begin to recoup their losses, they often breathe a sigh of relief *and then bailout*—thus canceling the chance for future profits.

How do you keep yourself invested for the long haul? Write down your stock-bond-cash combination and your stock-diversification mix. Make a note of the reasons you adopted this strategy and what sort of long-run returns and short-term losses you expect. Chapter 2 contains a worksheet that will assist you in determining how your investments are deployed and provides ample room for notes. When stocks next dive, take a moment to read what you wrote in quieter times. Without that reminder, an understanding of why you got into this scenario in the first place vanishes and investing becomes a short-term game.

With individual stocks, conviction is even more difficult, because mistakes are so much more common. You shouldn't, however, judge your stocks by day-to-day share-price movements. Instead, by writing down your three top reasons for owning a stock, such as a target earnings growth rate, reliable dividend increases or price earnings ratio. If any of those things change, it's an investment breaker, regardless of the stock price. If you just look at stock-price changes, you may make decisions that have nothing to do with your original conviction.

You don't want the performance of the market to make you think you made a mistake. If you're in small-cap funds and you underperform the large-cap indexes, you shouldn't use that as a reason to sell. Underperformance relative to comparable funds is more worrisome. But even then, I wouldn't become concerned unless a fund lagged behind its peers for a year to a year-and-a-half. I would become concerned if there was a change of fund manager or the fund's assets grew or shrank rapidly.

Mistake Number Six: Listen To Just One Adviser. Especially to their short-term advice. People on Wall Street are paid to have opinions. More than a few professionals will say the U.S. stock market is headed for big trouble at any given point in any given year. Let's say you believe this—to the point of selling all your stocks. Will the expert you followed then tell you when to get back into the market? Will that expert make up for any gains you forgo should the market rise rather than fall while you're on the sidelines?

• **Advice for those who listen to just one adviser:** If you are mulling an all-or-nothing market-timing decision based on somebody else's forecast, remember that in November 1995, almost no one on Wall Street predicted that Asia would blow up in 1997, that gold prices would drop to 14-year lows in 1999, or that the Dow would break through 10,000 in March of 1999, a 100 percent gain in just three-and-a-third years.

Mistake Number Seven: Don't Diversify. Perhaps the surest path to ruinous investment losses is to keep your assets concentrated in relatively few securities or classes of securities. Has your employer's stock been a stellar performer over the last few years? Great—but if that stock now accounts for half of your financial assets (in your retirement plan, for example), how would you feel if the price were to collapse.

• **Advice for not diversifying:** Effective diversification means using common sense to structure a portfolio of stocks and other financial assets (at a minimum, a cash cushion, and perhaps bonds) that makes sense for your risk tolerance. On the other hand, Warren Buffet, the historic value investor, once said about diversification, "that it's good for people who don't know what they're doing." If you're that confident in yourself, go back to the beginning and read "Mistake number one: Over-confidence."

Mistake Number Eight: Fall In Love And Marry Your Stocks. Loss of objectivity often leads to loss of money. It's healthy to respect well-run companies and want them to succeed especially when you own their stocks. But the closer you are to an investment, the less likely you are to see the big picture. And if that is changing to the disadvantage of your company, you may not realize it until it's far too late.

• **Advice for those who fall in love and marry their stocks:** Fast-growing, popular growth companies don't necessarily stay that way forever. You have to be able to recognize that when a company's prospects no longer justify the affection you may feel for the stock. Just think of the two blue chip stocks that were once blue-chip market leaders: "The B & O Canal Barge Co.", and the "U.S. Buggy Whip Company." (Note: These companies are examples that I created to make a point. I'm sure that research would uncover defunct companies that would have the same effect.)

Mistake Number Nine: Buy Lousy Companies Cheap. Master mutual-fund manager and investor Peter Lynch once put together a list of the "10 most dangerous things people say about stock prices." One of them was, "The stock-price is $3. What can I lose?" The answer, Lynch noted, is that you can lose 100 percent of your investment if the company ends up in bankruptcy. His point was that low-priced stocks often get that way for a good reason; because the company that issued the stock is poorly run and/or has bad business prospects.

• **Advice for those who buy lousy companies cheap:** You can outperform the Wall Street experts by investing in companies or industries you already know. Never invest in a company without understanding its finances. The biggest losses in stocks come from companies with poor balance sheets.

You have to know what you own and why you own it. "This stock is hot and bound to go up!" doesn't cut it. If you can't find any companies that are attractive, put your money in T-bills until you discover some.

This advice is good for those who don't yet use the Y-Process. When you learn about the Y-Process in Part Three, you'll be able to modify this advice appropriately.

Mistake Number Ten: Not Paying Attention To Costs. Maybe you've heard that line about the broker proudly showing off his new yacht to a friend. "And where are your customers' yachts?" the friend asks. Simply put, as an investor, you should get what you pay for. If you're paying high commissions for financial advice or investment transactions facilitated by an adviser, you should be earning a realistic return on the portfolio that adviser has constructed. If you're not, and you've had at least a year's experience to judge, it's probably time to find a new adviser. As for your mutual funds, have you ever looked at the management fees you pay?

• **Advice for not paying attention to costs:** If your fund's expense ratio is well above average, you should be getting well-above-average returns. Think of it this way: Every percentage point in expenses that your fund manager takes is a percentage point off your return—a loss to you, by any other name.

Mistake Number Eleven: Don't Worry About Taxes. Uncle Sam just loves it when you decide, for no good reason, to sell an investment at a gain in a *taxable account*. He takes his cut every time. Uncle reduced long-term capital-gains tax rates in 1997. Hold an investment for 12 months now, and any gain you realize when you sell will be taxed at a maximum of 20 percent, down from the maximum-possible 39.6 percent for capital gains, before the law was changed.

• **Advice For Those Who Don't Worry About Taxes:** But 20 percent is 20 percent of your money. If your capital gain is $1,000, that means Uncle Sam gets $200. Many states then take their own little piece of your action. Of course, when it's time to sell an investment, it's time to sell. But you should have a fundamental or strategic reason for selling. If you aren't sure whether to sell, maybe Uncle Sam's outstretched hand will help convince you to err on the side of holding-on and allowing the magic of compounding investment returns to work for you.

Mistake Number Twelve: Heed "Cold Calls." It's amazing that this process continues, but it does: Broker Smith, who you don't know, gets your phone number and calls. "How would you like a stock tip?" he asks. That's when you should give Broker Smith a tip: "You've got the wrong party!" Anyone who tries to sell you anything over the phone, with no knowledge of your financial situation or your risk tolerance, is a discredit to the professional investment business.

• **Advice for those who heed "cold calls":** If a broker or other financial adviser wants to meet you in person and talk about your total investment picture, it may be worth your time. But if you ever buy a security from someone you don't know and who doesn't know you, you deserve the losses you're likely to suffer. Unfortunately, the elderly are the most vulnerable. If you have a parent who is vulnerable to slick sales people, then keep a close eye out on their vulnerability and suggest that they check with you before they buy or sell stock or mutual-funds.

Mistake Number Thirteen: Get Caught Up In Wall Street's Hype. Newspapers, financial commentators and TV's financial broadcasters sell the hype about the market's breakthrough of Dow Jones's whole round numbers. The big one was on March 29, 1999 when the Dow broke 10,000. This just panders to the multi-zerophiliacs* and sells more copy and advertisement fee increases.

---

* A term coined by the author describing people who are lovers of "large, whole, round numbers."

On the day after the Dow broke 10,000, the morning newspapers declared, in their largest bold-font, "Dow hits 10,000 and stays there." Multi-colored charts and tables displaying "The march to 10,000" enhanced this.

The real risk to an investor getting caught up in this hype is that it could be *hazardous to your wealth*. It provides an excuse to neglect the careful, insightful strategic planning. Instead of pre-planned decisive steps, investors jump on the "can't-lose-bandwagon," making risky and imprudent snap decisions. Then one morning they wake up and find that the party is over.

• **Advice for those who get caught up in Wall Street's milestone, (deca-number) hype:** Before you do anything zany, consider "milestones" in their percentage equivalents. When the market breaks through 20,000, that will represent a 100 percent change from its 10,000 milestone. But, in the interim the Dow had to pass through other milestones, i.e., 11,000, 12,000, 17,000, 18,000 and 19,000. In terms of percentages, this series represents a magnitude growth in descending order: 10 percent, 9.1 percent,—6.3 percent, 5.9 percent and 5.6 percent, respectively. The reason? Future gains have a smaller percentage impact due to the Dow's higher levels.

Putting this numbers game in prospective, as recently as Oct. 20, 1987, the Dow had a *one-day gain* of 5.9 percent. Percentage-wise that's equivalent of the Dow going from 17,000 to 18,000 in one day. Can it happen? It's possible.

5

Benchmarking: Going Beyond
The S&P 500 Stock Index

FOR THE KNOWLEDGEABLE INVESTOR, BENCHMARKING IS CRITICAL TO MEASURING SUCCESS AND EVALUATING PROSPECTIVE INVESTMENTS.

How Do You Find The Right Benchmark And Interpret Returns?
Benchmarks are useful measurements for comparing performances of *individual mutual* funds with indexes that reflect similar investment categories. However, investors should be careful about comparing their total investment performance with a single benchmark. A diversified portfolio should consist of a mix of funds, with different styles and objectives. Under such circumstances, benchmarks become an effective way to measure the specific rates of return of the individual funds within your portfolio.

For investors trying to determine whether their respective investment returns are ahead or behind from one year to the next, may depend on the investor's dividend reinvestment policy. For example, from 1973 through 1998, *before* dividends were reinvested, the Wilshire 5000—which tracks the entire U.S. market—sports the best *cumulative* annual returns with

1,213%. This rate compares with 1,160% for the S&P 500 and 979% for the Dow Jones. However, if the dividends for these three indexes were reinvested, the average annual return for those 25-years would have been 13.6% for both the Dow and S&P 500, and 13.4% for the Wilshire 5000.

All Indexes Are Not Created Alike. The Dow is a price-weighted index of 30 stocks, meaning that changes in the value of high-priced stocks affect the value of the Dow more than changes in low-priced stocks do. On the other hand, the S&P 500 is weighted according to *market capitalization—* shares outstanding times the price of each stock.

This mathematical difference provides some strange outcomes. Since Disney's market capitalization is about eight times that of Union Carbide's, Disney's weight in the S&P 500—is eight times that of Union Carbide's. In the Dow, however, Union Carbide has roughly twice the weight of Disney because the price of Union Carbide's stock is twice that of Disney's. This inconsistency makes the Dow a questionable index. Some financial historians argue that the reason for the Dow's price weighting was that the Dow was created in 1896, when capitalization-weighting would have been too cumbersome for Charles Dow to calculate by hand.

Which Is The Best Stock Market Benchmark To Measure Market Performance? Table 5.1 indicates how the top three stock market benchmarks compare on an annualized basis through 1998.

Table 5.1 How The Three Stock-market Benchmarks
Compare On A Total Annual-Return Basis[2]

Index	One Year (1998)	3 Years[1] (Annualized)	5 Years[1] (Annualized)	10 Years[1] (Annualized)
DJIA	18.1%	23.8%	22.3%	18.8%
S&P 500	28.7%	28.3%	24.1%	19.2%
Wilshire 5000	23.4%	24.4%	21.8%	18.1%

1. Source: Wall Street Journal, Jan 4, 1999. (Lipper Inc.)
2. With dividends reinvested

Dueling Benchmarks—Dow vs. S&P 500 Vs. Wilshire 5000. In comparing benchmark indexes, six of one, half-dozen of the other. That's what many market watchers have customarily thought, until recently, when the Dow and the S&P 500 broke from their historical lockstep. The Dow probably has the highest name recognition of any market indicator. The Dow has been around since the 19th century. It tops most daily news stories on the stock market. But the Standard & Poor's 500 is probably more reliable as a market indicator because of its size—500 blue chip companies which include the 30 Dow companies. It is the principal barometer used by most Wall Street professionals and the more knowledgeable amateurs, because it reflects a broader swath of the market.

There have been esoteric debates about which gauge is the best to measure the market, but it probably doesn't matter which one is used. The Dow and S&P 500 performed about the same, that is, they customarily tracked one another. From 1990 through 1996, the Dow had average annual returns of 16.2 percent, versus 14.3 percent for the S&P. But, in the last five years, there has been a role reversal between the Dow and the S&P, where the S&P outperforms the Dow. This is illustrated by reviewing the results of Table 5.1. While the S&P returned 28.7 percent in 1998, with dividends reinvested, the Dow gained just 18.1 percent—an unusually large difference. That performance difference occurred after the previous year, when the S&P 500 returned 33.4 percent and the Dow returned 24.9 percent.

In hindsight, it's easy to determine what happened. In 1998, technology stocks soared, with Microsoft up 114.6 percent and Lucent Technologies skyrocketing to 175.9 percent. Stocks such as these are heavy "hitters" in a capitalization-weighted index influenced by companies with the highest value. For example, Microsoft is the largest company in the index, accounting for 4 percent of the S&P's value. So Microsoft's stunning gains had far more effect than if it were just one of 500 companies counted equally. It should be noted that Microsoft is also in the Dow.

Is It Possible To Profit From A Performance Difference Among The Three Indexes?
In 1998, the largest 50 companies in the S&P 500 accounted for 85 percent of its gains; the top 10 alone accounted for 42 percent. So a big upward swing by those heavyweights pushed the whole index up dramatically, even though hundreds of other stocks didn't do well. Indeed, 42 percent of S&P 500 stocks fell in price in 1998.

As illustrated in Table 5.1, the Wilshire 5000 underperformed the S&P 500 by five percentage-points in 1998—a 23.4% total return vs. the S&P's 28.8% return—although the Wilshire's return was a record return in its 25-year history. By contrast, the Wilshire's 5000 return beat the S&P's 500 return from 1975 through 1981—outperforming the S&P 500 by a full seven percentage points in 1979. Over the 25 years through 1998, the two indexes have delivered virtually identical 16.1% average annual returns.

How can an investor profit from performance differences between these two indexes? Obviously, by investing in the index that you expect will perform best. Is there a way to predict which index will outperform which? As William Shakespeare said, "There's the rub." In other words, there is no way of predicting the future based on past performance. That is why the Securities and Exchange Commission requires the following statement to be included in all fund prospectuses. "Past performance is no indication of future results."

Table 5.2 Benchmarking the Benchmarks.
(You can select a benchmark that best correlates with your mutual fund.)

Dow Jones Industrial Average (DJIA, or "Dow")	30 large industrial companies appropriate only for comparing	Owing to its narrow definition, it's funds indexed directly to it.
Dow Jones Transportation Average (DJTA)	20 stocks in the broadly defined transportation industry (airlines, trucking, rail, etc.)	Transportation sector funds
Dow Jones Utility Average (DJUA)	15 electric and gas utilities	Utility stock funds
Dow Jones Composite Average	65 stocks in the three basic Dow averages	None
Standard & Poor's 500 Index (S&P 500)	500 large industrial and utility companies	Large-capitalization-oriented stock funds
Standard & Poor's 400 Mid-Cap Index (S&P 400)	400 of the largest stocks, excluding the 500 stocks in the S&P 500	Mid-cap funds
Standard & Poor's 600 Small-Cap Index (S&P 600)	600 of the largest stocks after excluding the 900 stocks in the S&P 500 and S&P 400	Mid-cap and small-cap funds
Russell 1000 Index	The 1,000 largest-capitalization stocks in the U.S.	Large-cap and mid-cap funds
Russell 2000 Index	The 2,000 largest stocks excluding the Russell 1000 Index	Mid-cap and small-cap funds,
Russell 3000 Index	All 3,000 stocks in the Russell 1000 and 2000 indices	Total stock market funds
Value Line Average (VLA)	An equally weighted index of 1,900 stocks followed by the Value Line Investment Survey	Mid-cap and small-cap funds
Wilshire 5000 Index	All NYSE, Amex, and Nasdaq stocks	Total stock market fund
Nasdaq Composite Index	All of the several thousand stocks on Nasdaq	Over-the-counter funds
Nasdaq 100 Index	100 of the largest stocks on Nasdaq, heavily weighted toward technology	Too narrowly defined for most applications benchmarking
Morgan Stanley Capital International Europe Index (MSCI Europe)	All European stock markets	Diversified European funds
Morgan Stanley Capital International Select Emerging Markets Free Index (MSCI Emerging Markets)	Many developing country markets	Diversified emerging markets funds
Morgan Stanley Capital International Austral-Asia, Far East Index (MSCI EAFI)	All major stock markets outside the U.S.	Diversified international funds, Excluding emerging markets
Dow Jones World Stock Index	2,900 stocks in 34 countries, including 730 U.S. stocks	Diversified int'l & global funds

Comparing Fund Performance With The Predominant Market Indexes.

Because of the relatively rigid construction of market indexes and the differences between their performance and mutual fund portfolios, most professionals favor comparing fund performances to broad mutual fund peer groups. Thus, the S&P 500 is still the most widely used benchmark for measuring mutual fund performance.

Notwithstanding what most professionals prefer the S&P 500 is not an appropriate benchmark for the vast majority of funds. It is relevant only for comparing returns of mutual funds that invest in large capitalization* domestic stocks. To help the reader match up the right market index with their particular fund's style, Table 5.2, "Benchmarking the Benchmarks" summarizes the most popular indexes in use today.

Be Alert When Comparing Returns Of Popular Market Indexes With Fund Returns.

When measuring the performance of an investment in a mutual fund, it is important to consider the fund's distributions. Whenever a fund makes a distribution, its "net asset value" is reduced by precisely the amount of the distribution. Because the fund also fluctuates in value due to market changes on the day the distribution is deducted, the actual price change is usually different than the amount of the distribution. Ultimately, funds distribute nearly all profits and losses to investors, so a fund's net asset value could be unchanged over a period of time in which investors nevertheless made a considerable amount of money from the distributions.

Nearly all of the popularly published equity indexes have one significant, failing: The index's return is based on its price. This means that for an equitable apples-to-apples comparison, the investor must subtract from your fund's total return its income payout, e.g., dividends paid to the investor over the year.

---

* Firms whose net present value times the number of shares are greater than $2-billion. AKA large cap.

Many Funds Are Difficult To Classify. Although some funds almost defy classification, rating agencies, such as, Morningstar, Lipper, Value Line, and Mutual Funds magazine, classify funds into one or more peer groups. *The Wall Street Journal*, for example, publishes indexes of aggregate fund performance for ten equity fund groups and eleven bond fund sectors based on data supplied by Lipper Inc. All small-cap funds, for example, are grouped together, forming an index, not of small stocks, but of the small-cap funds.

Most investment advisors suggest using several sources, including Morningstar, *The Wall Street Journal*, and even a fund's returns, and the longevity of the portfolio manager.

There is a lot of misinformation in labeling mutual fund investment categories and styles. Some funds are difficult to classify because managers invest across categories. Other funds change their stripes as managers come and go, or as their sponsors strive to acquire and maintain marketable products. It is important for you to study the prospectus thoroughly to understand management goals. Then, it's important for you to compare the investor's own objectives to determine if the fund's strategy is reflected in the fund's portfolio. You should understand the differences between funds within the same peer group to make effective investment decisions.

Distinguishing between active and passive investing is an important criterion when choosing the best benchmark. When you consider a passively managed fund (i.e., an index fund), broad-based market benchmarks can be appropriate. For actively-managed investments—considering security selection, timing of purchases and sales, and possibly market timing—you need to pay more attention to the fund's peer group. It's important to determine whether the peer group's funds have similar investment objectives and asset holdings.

Table 5.3 Benchmarks for Mutual Fund Investors On A Total-Return Basis

Investment Objective	One Year 1998	3 Years* (Annualized)	5 Years* (Annualized)	10 Years* (Annualized)
DJIA (w/div)*	18.1%	23.8%	22.3%	18.8%
S&P 500 (w/div.)	28.7%	28.3%	24.1%	19.2%
Small-Co. Index Fund[1]	-2.6%	12.8%	12.9%	13.0%
Lipper Index-Europe	23.8%	22.4%	16.7%	NA
Lipper Index-Pacific	-3.0%	-10.1%	-6.7%	NA
Lipper L-T Gov't[2]	7.8%	6.3%	6.0%	7.9%
AVG. Stock Fund	14.5%	19.5%	17.4%	16.1%
AVG. Bond Fund	5.6%	6.4%	6.2%	8.4%

Source Wall Street Journal, Jan 4, 1999.
1 Vanguard tracks Russell 2000.
2 Includes government agency debt. (Source: Lipper Inc.)
* With dividends reinvested.

Table 5.4 How Lipper Fund Indexes Compare For 1998

Equity Indexes	Percentage Change
Capital Appreciation	19.99%
Growth Fund	25.65
Small Capitalization Fund	-0.85
Growth & Income Fund	13.58
Equity & Income Fund	11.78
Science and Technology Fund	46.77
International Fund	12.66
Balanced Fund	-12.80
Emerging Markets Fund	-26.87
Bond Indexes	**Percentage Change**
Corporate A-Rated Debt	7.27
U.S. Government	7.82
Intermediate Investment Grade	7.85
Short Term Invest. Grade	5.70
General Municipal Debt	5.61
High Yield Municipal Debt	5.50
Global Income	6.34

Benchmarking Your Mutual Fund. A rising tide lifts all boats, but not all mutual funds, as demonstrated in Tables 5.3 and 5.4. An examination of the spread between the best and worst performing mutual fund categories for 1998 shows a substantial difference. Table 5.3 provides a comparison of benchmarks for mutual fund investors on a total return basis for one, three, five and ten years. You should notice that it was very difficult to outperform the S&P 500 during these years.

This leads us to an alternate strategy that you should consider. If managed funds could not outperform the S&P 500 over the periods illustrated in Table 5.3, you should consider replacing your actively managed fund. How? By managing your own fund. The simplest way to do this is to purchase the S&P 500 stockindex and manage it using the Y-Process. You will learn in Part Three of this book the technique and investment strategy for doing this. Table 5.4 illustrates how different equity fund indexes compare. Each year you should stay tuned to the equity index which best matches your fund. If your fund does not match or exceed its Lipper Fund Index benchmark return, then you should consider switching to another fund in the fund family or transferring into another mutual fund family.

Other things being equal, and assuming a fund's portfolio matches up well with a particular market index and produces average performance in its class, you should expect it to slightly underperform the index. Underperformance occurs because fund returns are reduced by management fees, 12-1 charges, and operating costs. Furthermore, to facilitate shareholder redemptions and day-to-day portfolio transactions, funds typically hold a small portion of their portfolios in cash on which they earn only money market interest rates. Of course, better-performing funds in a particular category should beat their respective market benchmarks; any fund that consistently underperforms its benchmark by more than one or two percentage points, annualized, should be put on a "watch" list or sold.

A "Watch List" Provides Alerts When A Portfolio Declines. Deciding whether a mutual fund is worth holding is sometimes a difficult puzzle. You can't get a clear picture until the pieces come together. A "watch list" is a useful tool in providing this capability.

Investors should always pay attention to all their funds, but funds on a watch list require heightened attention. A watch list is a "yellow alert" status indication on a defensive scale in which increased risk developments spur the "red alert" of a sale. Listed here are seven events that should put your fund on the watch list.

• **Performance starts to lag.** Events that affect a fund eventually hit the bottom line, so lackluster returns raise the yellow flag. In Part Three, you will learn the mechanics of the Y-Process that immediately signal you when the fund crosses the "at-risk trip-wire."

• **The fund manager leaves.** Check into why the manager left. Check the new manager's objectives and goals. Once you are satisfied with the fund's management's goals and its performance comparison with its peer group, remove it from your watch list.

• **The fund changes its stripes.** For example, any time a small-cap fund becomes popular, assets tend to surge and the fund will outperform its peer group. In such an event, the fund is likely to drift toward buying medium-or large-cap companies. If a fund becomes too large, put it on the watch list to see whether it continues to do the job you bought it for in the first place.

• **The fund closes to new investors.** This action protects investors by keeping a fund true to its investment objectives. But sometimes it happens too late, after the fund has passed its optimum size. Cutting off new investors won't make the fund small and nimble again. If a fund closes, and you observe deterioration in performance, you have a potential reason for selling.

• **Portfolio characteristics change.** Whenever a fund does something out of character—e.g., hiking expense ratios or marketing fees, or doubling its turnover rate—proceed with caution. If this warning sign is coupled with other negative signals consider selling.

• **You receive a proxy statement that is seeking to change the fund.** Funds need investors permission to change their objective, the types of securities they buy and other stated goals. If an underperforming fund is asking to widen its investment scope, it may be a sign that the manger feels boxed in and is looking for a way out. If that happens you may want a way out, too.

• **Your objectives change.** Much of your satisfaction with a fund comes from its meeting your own needs, goals and comfort levels. The same fund that has been appropriate for you during the last 10 years may not be a good fit in the future. If your investment focus changes, make sure your funds fit in with your new agenda.

6

Why Indexing Makes Sense

WHEN DETERMINING WHETHER YOU SHOULD BE IN A TRADITIONAL MUTUAL FUND OR A PASSIVE INDEX FUND, THERE IS NO RIGHT ANSWER. CHOOSE WHICHEVER BEST SUPPORTS YOUR GOALS, PERFORMANCE EXPECTATIONS AND INVESTMENT STYLE.

How Does Indexing Work? Today, there are thousands of mutual funds from which to choose. If you are attracted to a disciplined and predictable investment method, there are many mutual fund companies who offer an unparalleled choice of U.S. stock index-funds to meet a wide variety of investment objectives.

All of U.S. stock index funds track a specific market index and each allows you to implement a well-defined strategy and style for your own investments—at a fraction of the cost of the typical mutual fund. While each has its own precise and consistent objective, they all share a common strategy—seeking to match the investment performance of a specific index, or market benchmark.

A traditional mutual fund buys and sells securities based on the fund manager's judgments about which stocks are likely to provide the greatest return to investors. An index fund, on the other hand, simply buys a large number (or all) of the securities listed in an index—seeking to duplicate that index's performance.

The traditional "active" approach typically gives a fund manager latitude in managing its holdings. As a result, investors in these funds are often not entirely sure how their money is being invested at a given moment. Also, the fund's performance, which is dependent on the adviser's strategies and tactics, comes at a significant yearly cost: typically 1% to 2% or more of assets invested.

Indexing's "passive" approach is more objective and predictable, and available for as little as one-sixth the yearly cost. As its name implies, index investing relies on indexes that combine groups of stocks to measure the performance of an overall market or specific market segment.

By its nature, indexing emphasizes broad diversification, minimal trading activity, and razor-thin costs. As a result, index investors benefit from a reduction of certain investment risks, the possibility of lower taxable distributions, and the ability to keep a higher percentage of investment returns.

The Dominance Of Actively-Managed Funds.
In August 1962, the University of Pennsylvania's prestigious Wharton School prepared an exhaustive study of mutual funds. The study's conclusion indicated that performance records varied considerably but, *on average*, they conformed to the market as a whole.

However, more recently, in June 1999, in a comprehensive analysis by researchers at the discount brokerage firm Charles Schwab & Co., concluded that just 17 percent of actively-managed *large-cap* funds beat the unmanaged-S&P 500 Index over the ten years through 1998. The Index's 10-year annualized return delivered an astonishing 19.21 percent. Whereas, according to Chicago's Morningstar Inc., all actively managed diversified U.S. stock funds returned 15.6 percent a year over the same

10-year period. Managers of U.S. stock funds didn't just lag behind the market they were essentially humiliated.

Results of both studies suggest that mutual funds have potentially advantageous attributes that make them worthy of elements of investment portfolios. Key advantages are diversification, liquidity and, professional management. However, management is indeed "professional" only if it generates a "realistic" return on an investment portfolio relative to the risks assumed. Unfortunately, over those same 10-years, these "professional" managers were little better than "amateur" investors were. Somewhat less than one-in-four of *all active-fund managers* actually earned their salary and bonus'.

Choosing The Right Mutual Fund. Throughout the 1990s the market has undergone a fundamental change. Because of access to new technologies, investors have taken greater control of their portfolios. There are unprecedented information and investment choices available. The major issue with mutual funds is how do you select the right one for you. The elements of your financial portfolio should be a mirror of your investment nature—the one thing that has not changed. However, with so many financial choices it may be trickier than ever to match style with substance. If you are going to choose a mutual fund I suggest you choose a no-load fund. Next, you should choose a fund that matches your style. Whether you are an aggressive-, active- or prudent-investor, there are investment strategies that you should consider to achieve realistic returns while preserving your capital when buying funds (or index stock). If you are unsure of which style of investor you are, I suggest that you take the *risk test*, which can be found, at the end of Chapter 1.

The Stock Index-Fund Craze. While the overwhelming majority of mutual-fund assets are actively managed, index-funds have become more popular through the 1990s because so many fund managers failed to beat the market's S&P 500 benchmark. The 10-year annualized return of the S&P 500 index-based funds through 1998 were nearly as astonishing as the index they track. Most index-funds are lean operations that, on average, have an expense ratio of just 0.54 percent of assets, compared with 1.45 percent for the average fund with a stock-picking manager and research assistants.

The indexing craze has been helped by the growing frustration that many mutual fund owners feel as the tax-reporting season approaches. Actively managed funds can wallop investors with large capital-gains tax bills, especially if high turnover is part of a manager's operating style. Customarily, index fund managers buy or sell only as investors come and go, or to adjust for changes in the index itself, so their capital-gains distributions are relatively low. For investors, this distinction means that it is wise to include actively managed funds in their tax-sheltered retirement portfolios.

An index fund that matches the entire U.S. market. For the broadest possible diversification in a U.S. stock index fund, consider buying a portfolio that tracks the Wilshire 5000 stock index. Vanguard's fund, which debuted in 1992, is by far the largest of a group of funds designed to track the performance of the entire stock market as measured by the Wilshire 5000 stock index. Other companies that offer a total stock market index fund include Fidelity, Charles Schwab, T. R. Price, and Wilshire Associates.

Like the market itself, these funds are dominated by large-cap stock, but they allow an investor to get exposure to the approximately 25% of the market not in the S&P 500. Wilshire 5000 is a great way for you to start investing and get broad market exposure while making only one minimum investment. It is the real-world application of modern portfolio theory (which you will learn about in the next chapter).

• **How does a fund go about buying the stocks of the entire U.S. market?** A casual investor might think these funds own every stock in the Wilshire 5000. They do not. Instead, the funds use computer programs to select a representative sample of the stocks that have the same exposure to risk factors and produce the same return as the entire index.

More than 7,000 U.S. companies are now in the Wilshire 5000 index, whose name is based on the size of the U.S. equity market in 1974, when the index was created. These index funds invest in a selection of stocks that resemble the total market in terms of industry weightings, average market capitalization, price-earnings ratio, book value, dividend yield and other characteristics. In comparison, an S&P 500-composite index fund does hold all the stocks in the S&P 500 in about the same proportion as in the index itself. This technique is called *replication*. Complete replication of the target is the ideal, but sometimes that is not practical and sometimes it just doesn't make sense. While replication creates a proportional copy of an index, sampling recreates the index's fundamental profile with far fewer stocks. It still takes five hundred million calculations at the end of each trading day to keep Vanguard's Total Stock Market index fund on track.

While replication creates a proportional copy of an index, sampling recreates the index's fundamental profile with far fewer stocks. The number of stocks held in these funds varies from around 1,100 in T. Rowe's Total Equity Market to more than 3,100 in Vanguard's Total Stock Market. Of these 3,100 stocks, the top 1,000 represent 90% of the total market. The rest of the portfolio, which represents 6,500 or so stocks in the index, is selected by computer program.

A Recent Development: Stock-Exchange Traded Funds. Although index funds provide you a disciplined and predictable method of meeting your investment objectives, with the reduction of certain investment risks and at a small percentage of the cost of a conventional mutual fund, there is

another approach to buying the market. This new approach buys a selected market index through a recent development called Stock exchange traded funds (SEFs) and sometimes also called index-stock.

Simply put, a SEF is a basket of stocks, grouped so that they can be traded like shares of common stock. SEFs provide dividends like ordinary stock. And, like stock, they can be held for either the short or long term. How a particular SEF tracks the market is determined by its composition, the percentage weight of each component, and the method of calculating the index. For example, one of the oldest SEFs is the SPDR* pronounced spider. Spiders are traded on the American Stock Exchange under the trading symbol SPY. Since the Spiders are capitalization weighted any change in price of any one its 500 stock-components, influences the index in proportion to the relative market value of that firm's outstanding shares. The market value of the S&P 500 firms is equal to about 80 percent of the value of all stocks listed on the New York Stock Exchange.

• **S&P 400 mid-cap stock exchange-traded stock.** This Stock exchange-traded stock represents the "middle" of the market. Like the S&P 500, the S&P 400 is traded on the AMEX as a SPDR under the trading symbol MDY. Like the SPYs, MDYs are not static. Standard and Poor's Co. add and delete stocks as conditions change, but a given stock would never be included in both the SPY and the MDY.

• **Nasdaq 100 index.** In March of 1999, the Nasdaq 100 index was introduced and is traded on the AMEX under the trading symbol QQQ, sometimes called "cubes" by industry mavens. This stock-market traded fund is rebalanced annually so that the index reflects 100 of the largest and most active domestic, non-financial common stocks listed by its parent, the Nasdaq Composite index. The cubes are a capitalization-weighted index and normally have an 85 to 95 percent correlation to their parent index. However, in the heady days of 1999, when the Nasdaq Composite increased

---

* Standard and Poor's Depository Receipts, (pronounced Spiders) ticker symbol, SPY, were created in Feb. 1993.

its seven-plus-year lead over the Dow, soaring 85 percent, a record gain for U.S. stock index, the cubes outperformed its parent by sixteen percent.

• **International stock exchange-traded stock.** Since 1990, combined U.S. and international indexed mutual fund assets have increased greater than 3,000 percent. Investing only in the U.S. market, an investor misses the opportunities achievable from 60 percent of the worlds equity market (WEBS). WEBS are designed to give U.S. investors exposure to specific international equity markets through a diversified portfolio of stock for each foreign country selected.

The WEBS* Index-fund, Inc., an index-fund contains many of the largest foreign markets and their major local market Stock exchange-traded stock, such as Germany's DAX and Japan's Nikkei 225. Chapter 11 provides more detail concerning the existing WEBS, seventeen countries, their local market index and the symbol used to trade these WEBS on the American Stock Exchange. Investing in any of these foreign countries WEBS would provide investment results that correspond to the price and yield performance of their publicly traded securities in the aggregate as compiled by Morgan Stanley Capital International Index. The intermediate investor should be advised that these investments are purchased through a simple stock trade and are free from the complexities, but not the risks, of foreign investing.

Advantages Of Investing In Stock Exchange-Traded Funds.
While many investors have similar objective (or goals), very few are exactly alike. Certain SEFs that are traded on the American Stock Exchange—also known as Index-stocks—provide each investor the opportunity to select the index that best matches their investment style and meets their investment objectives. They can be used for asset allocation, for following index-stock momentum trends, or for balancing your portfolio—with

* World Equity Benchmark Shares

convenience, efficiency and affordably. Because stock exchange-traded stocks are easy to trade, they provide the investor with an ideal vehicle for portfolio management. In Part Three, the investor will learn how to assess and manage SEFs risk using the Y-Process.

• **Tracking and trading portfolios throughout the day.** Unlike mutual funds, the investor won't have to wait until the end of the trading day to purchase or sell stock exchange-traded stock shares. This real-time trading feature on the AMEX provides the investor with the power to react swiftly to market changes. Another advantage is that the investor will always be able to obtain up-to-the-minute share prices electronically, from your broker or financial adviser.

• **Diversification.** Buying shares of different SEFs is one way to add important diversification and to reduce risk in your stock portfolio. With stock exchange-traded stock, the investor can hedge his portfolio against the potential decline of different market segments under varying economic conditions. Diversifying across several index stock types may help the investor to further reduce risk and reallocate assets.

• **Index tracking.** Unlike actively managed equity funds that attempt to outperform the market, each stock exchange-traded stock seeks to provide investment results that correspond to the price and yield performance of its related market index.

• **Lower costs.** Stock exchange-traded stock are designed for investors who seek a relatively low-cost "passive" approach for investing. With lower operating expenses and management fees. Typically, a stock exchange-traded stock has net expenses of approximately .2 percent of its net asset value. There are no sales loads on Stock exchange-traded stock but ordinary brokerage commissions do apply.

• **Tax efficiency.** Because stock exchange-traded stocks are designed to closely track their respective underlying indexes, they are less likely than actively-managed portfolios to trade securities which can result in high capital gain distributions. The average stock exchange-traded stock portfolio has a turnover rate of 4 percent per year. Indeed, underlying Indexes will generally only sell securities to reflect changes in the composition of the Index.

Additionally, since stock exchange-traded shares are sold through exchange trading, they generally do not require the sale of stocks and the generation of capital gains that is required by mutual funds in effecting cash redemption.

• **Quarterly dividends.** As with stock, your stock exchange-traded stock may pay the investor quarterly cash dividends representing dividends accumulated on the stocks held by the respective underlying Index, less fees and expenses of the Stock exchange-traded shares. There also may be opportunities for dividend reinvestment.

• **Margin eligibility.** Stock exchange-traded shares can be bought on margin, generally subject to the same terms that apply to common stocks.

• **Short selling on a "downtick."** A key feature for active/aggressive investors is that stock exchange-traded stock can be sold short at any time during trading hours. Selling a stock short must be done on a "downtick," that is, the sale of the security must take place at a price that is lower than the price of the previous (regular-way) transaction.

• **Convenience.** Stock exchange-traded stocks offer the investor the convenience of investing in portfolios of stocks included in domestic indexes, foreign indexes and sector stock indexes. The composition of these indexes is readily available from your broker, your financial adviser or electronically from the Amex web site www.amex.com—to determine how your money is invested and how your investment is performing.

Conclusion. Some financial advisers recommend that a category of funds, which would make a nice fit with index-funds are the increasingly popular "concentrated" funds, also known as "select" or "focus" funds; typically they hold 35 or fewer stocks and may invest more than ten percent of fund assets in a single name. Select-funds invest to deliver significantly higher returns. Proven stock pickers have recently delivered market-beating results with concentrated funds. Part Three contains two chapters (11 and 12) which provide additional data, for the advanced investor, on understanding the advantages and limitations of including select funds as part of their portfolio.

With time, new investment vehicles, such as select-stock portfolios, will proliferate the market place to feed investors' insatiable appetite for new and innovative products. With so many financial choices, it will become easier than ever to match each investor's style with substance.

PART THREE

ASSISTING SOPHISTICATED INVESTORS TO PRESERVE THEIR CAPITAL, WHILE AT THE SAME TIME, ENHANCING THEIR RETURNS THROUGH JUDICIOUS USE OF THE Y-PROCESS.

(Chapters 7 through 12)

Preface: This part of the book is written for the sophisticated investor. As an experienced investor, you have probably developed the habit of investing in stocks regularly, determined your tolerance for risk and, as a result, have developed a personalized, diversified portfolio. You've met your short-term goals and possibly your interim goals as well. Now, you're in the real wealth building part of your long-journey—obtaining financial security to support a comfortable retirement. There is a problem gnawing at you though; a fear of encountering a bear on your journey that will maul your goal.

Caveat: Part Three develops the Y-Process, a stock market model that forecasts crucial market turns enabling the investor to reduce risk and enhance returns. The Y-Process synthesizes the precursors of change in the market's trend, that is, whether a bull market or bear market is in process. Its greatest value for the investor is its ability to detect the transition from bull to bear, or from bear to bull, very close to major crucial turning points.

The Y-Process was developed using statistical mathematical analysis of 70-years of Standard and Poor's 500 data. The Y-Process signals the investor when to enter the market and when to sell the market. The statistics over the past 70-years indicate that, on average, there have been seven turning points per year. However, this does not mean that Y-Process calls *every* turn with total accuracy. Examination of historic "transition data" indicates that there have been anomalies, that is, occurrences of "false alarms" and "whipsaws." Even with these anomalies, statistically over each year, the Y-Process works very well as evidenced by the fact that in the past 70 years, it has *never* had a losing year.

7

Taking A Bite Out
Of Your Retirement

*PRESERVING CAPITAL WITH REALISTIC RETURNS REQUIRES A STRATEGY THAT
ALERTS THE INVESTOR THAT A SEVERE BEAR MARKET IS ON ITS WAY*

Introduction For The Advanced Investor. This chapter is the first in a series of five chapters in Part Three. In these chapters, you will learn about a risk-management investment strategy based on the "Y-Process." This strategy will guide you in your portfolio selection and management that will enhance returns, reduces risk, anticipate market downturns, and call market turns. I will provide evidence of a market timing/trading strategy that works for stock portfolios and stock mutual funds. It gets you out of the market in time to avoid most of the bear market and back into the market to take advantage of most of the recovery. The consequence of this strategy is to *1) reduce the severity of the drop on your stock portfolio, 2) put you in T-bills while you're waiting to return to the recovering market, and 3) shorten the recovery time to your portfolio's value before the bear attacked.*

111

Introducing you to the Kodiac-grizzly. Chances are a prolonged downturn will maul the stock market sometime during your quest to save for your retirement. Are you prepared or will it wreck your retirement plans? The last thing anyone saving for retirement wants to think about is a bear market. Investors dread the prospect of wealth wiped out in a ravenous, long-lasting decline like those that savaged portfolios in the 1930s and 1970s. Would you be able to anticipate or recognize a bear if you bumped into one? Not that kind of bear; I'm talking about an honest-to-goodness *Kodiak-grizzly bear* stock market.

Market Phases. The stock market normally goes through three phases before being officially declared a bear market—a loss of more than 20 percent. First a *routine decline*—5 percent or greater, next a *moderate correction*—10 percent or greater and finally a *severe correction*—15 percent or greater. Oh, there are some rare occasions when the market will slice right through these phases like a hot knife through butter—some cataclysmic occurrence that will cause the bottom to fall out of the market. It's usually the uncertainty associated with these calamitous events that cause the free-fall. For example, the assassination of a president, or a terrorist bombs the congress while in session. However, the recovery from these types of events is usually quite rapid. Since normal stock market bears start with a *routine decline*, the chance of this turning into a bear market is only about nine-percent, whereas approximately one-quarter of *moderate corrections* become a bear and almost 60 percent of all *severe corrections* become bear market.

Is the present bear market barometer obsolete? Historically, the stockbrokers on Wall Street defined a bear market when the Dow Jones Industrial Average dropped by 20 percent or more from its previous high. This paradigm dates back to the beginning of the century when brokers used ticker tape to transmit stock prices. However, there's a problem with this antiquated definition. As the market grew from a few hundred companies to well over 7,000 firms as it is today, a bear market *in stocks* should represent more than just the 30 companies of the Dow.

If asked, most financial analysts, brokers and money managers would agree that the standard for the U.S. stock market is the Standard & Poor's 500 composite-stock index, which, by the way, contains the Dow 30. Unfortunately, the "Wall Street" pros have not broken the paradigm of using the Dow 30 as the proxy for determining when a bear market occurs. I believe that the 500 companies in the S&P are more in tune with and better reflect the total stock market's impact on stock-portfolios. I favor changing the "official" definition of a bear market as a severe downturn in the S&P 500 of greater than 20 percent from its previous peak.

Should a bear market be more than just a number? There is a problem with using just a number for the definition of a bear market. As an example, in 1998, while the sell-off in stocks from mid-July through August was steep and violent, the question was whether it truly marked the end of the bull market that began almost eight years previously. The answer wasn't simple. On the last day of August, the Dow's closing low was down 19.3 percent from its high. Although the Dow fell through the 20 percent level briefly the following day, it never did stay down for the count. That intraday low turned out to be it's lowest point. The good news in August of 1998 was that much of the decline had already happened and the conditions for a severe, multi-year wealth-destroying event turned out to be just a scare.

How would you feel if the market fell 20.5 percent and then returned to where it started in a matter of weeks? To many investors it wouldn't feel like a bear market. Bear markets come in different colors. The 33.5 percent drop in the bear of 1987 only took *four months* to its nadir, but dragged on for about *two years* before recovering most of its losses. At the beginning of the following decade, the bear market of 1990 was a much tamer bear—its downturn to hit the minus 20 percent mark and took the same time to its trough in 1987—*four months*. But, this 1990 bear made a new high only four months after it's trough—hence, it's stagnation time was one-third as long 1987 which had the effect of muzzling the bear.

Far more damaging are bear markets like 1929 and 1973, which brought on years of stagnation. That type of gut-wrenching bear market requires something fundamental to go wrong in the global economy.

The mood swings of investor sentiment who are not Y-Process users. In the decade of the 1990s, the relative toothlessness of bear markets has helped make bullishness practically a religion. Investors have been lured by more than a decade of extraordinary 19-percent average annual return in the market. People "tune-in and turn-on" to the simple story—today that story is that stocks *always* outperform other investments as evidenced by the returns of the 1990s. In the phenomenal bull market's rosy glow, investors increasingly forget normal measures of value. "Dividend yields don't matter much these days," you hear people say. People believe that "Alan Greenspan* and the Fed will prevent us from getting into trouble." Ask investors in the 1990s what they'd think of a drop in the stock market, and most would exclaim, "Buying opportunity!"

A strong psychological shift is required for an investor to switch from a bullish to a bearish sentiment. A shift in feeling really comes when stock prices go down and *stay down*. When that happens, expectations of what stocks will return over time are lowered considerably. There's a transformation in investor's perception since "stocks don't work well anymore." Fear sets in; people start shifting away from stocks into other types of assets, such as bonds. That sort of grizzly market brings out the tremulous people who say, "this is the beginning of the end." The longer the recovery time, the greater the chances that fear turns into terror. Each investor

---

* Alan Greenspan is the Chairman of the Federal Reserve Board, sometimes referred to as the Fed.

has his own pain-threshold. Mutual fund statistics demonstrate that there is high correlation between a severe market downturn and the number of "buy-and-holders" who throw in the towel—move out of stocks and into bonds, money market or the equivalent.

Investor psychology can change on a short-term basis and create a lot of negative market volatility. However, a real Kodiak-grizzly reflects not only *a fundamental* change in investor psychology, but in economic and broad-based market deterioration; it takes time to determine that change. I believe that bear markets need to be rated not only by the *depth* of the drop, but also by the *time of recovery* to the market's previous peak. Table 7.2 contains a list of this century's *major* bear markets and their recovery times from market's low through to the market's previous peak. The worst case recovery time occurred in "the great crash of 1929." In this crash, it took until November of 1954, greater than 25 years, for the faithful "buy-and-hold" investor's stock value to return to its previous peak.

The Bear's Bite. You may be part of the stream of investors that has plowed hundreds of billions of dollars into stock or stock mutual-funds since the stock market crash of October 1987. If so, the only serious market downturn you experienced is the bear market of 1990. What makes the bear market bite particularly dangerous is that so many investors base their future expectations on recent history. Between July 16 and October 11 of 1990, the S&P index declined about 20 percent, an unpleasant trend but not a severe bear market. Compared to some of the grizzlies of the past, 1990 was a Teddy-bear-market, a short-lived and relatively mild downturn. Since 1900 there have been 29 bear markets; since 1933, 12 bear markets have come and gone, and since 1960, seven bears have attacked.

To get a reality check on bear markets lets review a little of stock market history. There's a technical term—"regression to the mean"—which statisticians use to describe a middle point between extreme values; in other words, new values tend to revert to the "expected value." Applying the *regression to the mean* concept, let's see what dangers may lie in the bullish expectations of the 90s, for investors in the next century

If the reader examines Table 7.1, it contains a summary of how frequently stock market declines have occurred since 1900, how deep they have been, and how long they have lasted. Statistically, the table illustrates that a bear is likely to strike every three years—although in recent history it's been closer to five years—bear markets last about one year (in recent history it's more like two and three-quarter years). On average, typically bears take a bite of approximately 35 percent out of the market (in recent history about 31 percent).

Table 7.1 Comparison Of This Century's Market Losses (1900-1998)

Market Loss Attributes	Decline (5 percent or more)	Moderate Correction (10 percent or more)	Severe Correction (15 percent or more)	Bear Market (20 percent or more)
Number of times since 1900	319	107	51	29
How often to expect this	About 3 times a year	About once a year	About once every 2 years	About every 3 years
Average loss before decline ends	11 percent	19 percent	27 percent	35 percent
Average length	40 days	109 days	217 days	364 days
Chance of decline turning into a bear market	9 percent	27 percent	58 percent	100 percent

Note: Averages are means. Days are calendar days, including weekends.
Source: Ned Davis Research, Inc., WSJ Statistics, as modified by the author for the severe correction of July through October, 1998.

For those, who no longer remember, the bottom fell out of the Dow—a free fall of 48 percent from 381.2 on 3 Sept. 1929, to 198.7 on Nov. 13 1929. Then the Dow rallied back 48 percent to 294.1 by April 17, 1930—only to melt-down a mind-numbing 86 percent over the next two years, finally bottoming out at 41.2 on July 8, 1932.

Since the great crash of 1929 the stock market has sustained rather mild bears in comparison. A review of the bear markets since 1960 indicates that we have had seven bears. On average they lasted 11 months, and each cost the investor about 30 percent. As bad as that seems, it pales in comparison with the most severe bear in postwar history: 1973-74. On January 11, 1973, the S&P 500 closed at an all-time high of 120.24. After a grinding downturn that persisted for almost two years; it finally bottomed on December 6, 1974, at 65.01. For comparison, in Dec. of 1998, a similar 48.2 percent loss from the market's peak (approximately 1,200) would send the S&P index spiraling down to about 620. In terms of the popular Dow average, which peaked near 9300, it would have dropped like a rock down a well to 4817.

The anguish and cost of following a bear "down the tubes." Tragically, I believe that the investment strategy of "buy-and-hold" is more myth than reality. Most buy-and-hold investors start with good intentions, but often, suffering through severe decline, they usually panic and sell. Sick over their losses, some never return, while others wait months or years before coming back. As a result, they miss the entire post-bear advance.

Then, there are the "buy-and-hold-forever" investors. These people are the ones whose slogan is "Stay cool—each time the market takes a dive it recovers *and* goes on to new highs." True,—but buy-and-hold-forever investors don't do very well during these recoveries *because instead of earning new profits, they're making up past loses.* A case in point; in the previous 1973-74 bear market, it would take a 96 percent gain to recover lost capital, even neglecting opportunity costs. On average, this recovery would take about 7.6 years at 9 percent compounded annually.

Table 7.2 contains those major bear markets in this century which really clawed the buy-and-holders and took a major bite out of their retirement plans and cost them significant profits. In the end, for "buy-and-hold-forever" investors, the real pain of a bear's bite is how long it takes to *recover* from that bite. As a simple example of the catastrophic impact that a bear market can have on your retirement plans, I present the following case: If your portfolio dropped 50 percent, it would have to *double*—a 100 percent increase—to make it back to the previous peak value. This doubling takes time and that time is just to *recapture* your lost capital—during this time you lose potential capital gains. Now you can better understand the cliché "time is money"—the time it takes to make back what you already made is called "opportunity cost." This is why investors should be *bear-shy*; be out of the market during severe corrections and ensconced in T-bills or the equivalent, e.g., money markets. In the chapters that follow, I will tell you how to recognize the approach of a Kodiak bear.

Table 7.2 Analyzing This Century's Major Bear Markets

DATE OF PEAK	S&P 500 DECLINE (%)	MONTHS TO TROUGH	YEARS TO RETURN TO LAST PEAK
July 16, 1990	-19.9	4	0.68
Aug. 25, 1987	-33.5	4	1.9
Nov. 28, 1980	-27.1	21	0.96
Sept. 21, 1976	-19.4	18	2.9
Jan 11, 1973	-48.2	22	7.5
Dec. 3, 1968	-36.1	18	2.8
Feb. 9, 1966	-22.2	8	1.3
Dec. 12, 1961	-28.0	6	2.7
May 29, 1946	-28.1	20	4
Sep. 3, 1929 (Great crash)	-47.9 *	2	25.2

* DJIA value. Eventually, the Dow fell 89 percent by July 8, 1932.
Source: Ned Davis Research, Wall Street Journal Statistics, 11/12/98

8

The Schools Of
Strategic Investing

THERE ARE THREE SCHOOLS OF STOCK MARKET INVESTING AND EACH IS AT ODDS WITH THE OTHERS BECAUSE EACH BELIEVES ONLY THEIR PERSUASION IS THE TRUE WAY TO ATTAIN INVESTORS' NIRVANA,—CONSISTENTLY OUTPERFORMING THE MARKET. THERE IS NO OPTIMUM INVESTMENT STRATEGY. EVEN THE BUY-AND-HOLD-FOREVER INVESTOR IS A CLOSET MARKET TIMER.

The Elements of Successful Investing. Many people invest because they want their money to grow, conservatively and intelligently, and because they are confident in their own judgment. If you consider yourself one of these people—and you should—this chapter contains suggestions that will assist you in becoming a more proficient and successful investor. For example, one of the most difficult tasks for most investors is to build, manage and measure the effectiveness of a stock market portfolio; a portfolio that is designed to meet their objectives, goals and stay within their risk tolerance. If you have reached this level of competence then you have mastered the science of "strategic market investing."

Strategic market investing is the procedure of creating, managing and measuring the effectiveness of your stock portfolio. To be an accomplished strategic investor you must know the answers to these four essential questions: "*What* securities should I select?," "*When* should I buy them?," "*When* should I sell them?," and finally, "*How well* did my portfolio perform?" Historically, there have been three different investment approaches—or *schools*—that sophisticated investors use to answer the four questions of strategic market investing. They are the schools of 1) *fundamental analysis*, 2) *technical analysis*, and 3) *efficient markets*. Each school approaches the question of security selection and market timing differently. As for the question of how well your portfolio performed, this is a function of the risk that you are prepared to take to obtain your desired return.

Whether you are a savvy stock market investor or an investor who would like to improve your investing skills, you should determine which school you belong to. In some cases, you may decide that you have multiple diplomas. After reading this chapter you may have second thoughts and may want to switch affiliations to better meet your financial goals, objectives and risk tolerance.

• **How well have the professional money managers performed over the years?** Let's take a page out of how professional money managers measure their performance. Professional managers of equity (stock) portfolios who use either the school of technical analysis or use the fundamental approach have a common goal to stock selection. They try to outperform the "market," that is, to achieve increases in a portfolio's value that exceed those of the market as a whole. For professionals who don't *actively* manage their portfolio, they usually buy market indexes or the market benchmark. Here, two primary representative stock indexes or benchmarks measure market swings. The benchmark most widely followed by the general public is the Dow (DJIA) of 30 blue-chip stocks. But most professionals use the S&P 500 composite stock Index as their benchmark to measure their management skills. By most measures, a manager who can beat the S&P 500 Index has had a successful year.

Mutual fund managers, independent investment advisers, bank trust departments and other professional investors follow hundreds of companies, employ staffs of analysts and economists, and use elaborate computerized trading techniques to beat the S&P 500 performance—most of them fail. Over the years, on average, greater than 85 percent of all mutual fund managers fail to beat the performance of the "plain vanilla" S&P 500 index each year; and, they are not the same managers every year. For example, according to Lipper Analytical Services, only 3.5 percent of all open-end equity funds outperformed the market (as measured by the S&P 500 index) from the end of 1993 to the end of 1998. Over the decade that ended in 1998, only 10 percent of the funds outperformed the market and this was the decade that had the longest bull market in history.

The message is clear: If you buy a mutual fund the chances are you will do significantly worse than the S&P 500. Whatever their success, managers use variations of two basic investment approaches (schools): "fundamental analysis," and "technical analysis." There is a third school but it does not require an active manager. I call this the school of "passive management." The balance of this chapter explores the advantages and limitations of these three schools as an approach for strategic market investing.

The School Of Fundamental Analysis. Investors who use fundamental analysis to buy (or sell) stock are called "fundamentalists." Fundamentalists come in two groups: the first is interested in *value investing*. Value fundamentalists analyze companies, industries, and the economic and market environments to identify stocks that are "undervalued" at their current market prices. The other group tries to identify companies with high-growth potential before that potential is reflected in the market value. Investors who use this approach are called *growth* fundamentalist.

• **The value fundamentalist group.** Value fundamentalists examine every "nook and cranny" of a company's financial statement. Among other things, they evaluate companies based on some combination of earnings momentum, relative price strength, price earnings (PE)/growth ratios, cash flows, dividend yields, revisions of analysts' earnings estimates, valuation levels and their earnings prospects in the context of their industry. The purpose of this detailed analysis is to get an idea of the stock's real worth. If that is significantly below the stock's market value, the value fundamentalist concludes that the stock has no significant downside risk and will eventually will rise to its "proper" market value. The legendary Warren Buffet set an all-time record by compounding money at 22 percent for 20 years as a value investor.

With the thousands of companies to review, evaluation of these financial statements is a monstrous task to accomplish manually. Value fundamentalists who are computer proficient may construct a computer program model to perform this task; or, they may hire a "quant" (computer programmer) to construct an elaborate computer model to account for various economic, corporate, or market factors. The increase in computing power has allowed for an *unemotional*, statistical analysis of a huge volume of fundamental information. The model can be made to rank stock from best to worst based on expected performance, theoretically removing subjective biases and other limitations that humans might bring to the process. Value fundamentalists may go a step further with another computer program, the "terminator," which eliminates the weak companies and builds a portfolio that conforms to pre-specific risk factors. The question has been asked, "Are there limits to the complexity of models one can build?" The answer is, "Cost and time are the only limits to building computer models that filter the data to meet specific requirements."

• **The growth fundamentalists group.** The growth fundamentalist seeks out companies that are expected to enjoy rapid growth based on the anticipated earnings growth of shares that are "undervalued." These companies are usually, although not always, younger, smaller companies in emerging industries that carry a higher degree of risk than established companies. They usually do not pay big dividends, since their earnings are reinvested to finance their rapid growth. The growth fundamentalists have their legend as well; the celebrated Peter Lynch, formerly of Fidelity's Magellan Fund, who garnered average annual returns of 29 percent compounded over a ten-year period.

Growth companies require meticulous and constant analysis. There are dramatic gains to be made in some growth stocks, although more efficient, computerized markets have reduced the number of what Lynch called ten-baggers—but risk increases significantly as well.

• **How well does fundamental analysis work.** It is safe to assume that at least 90% of all stock research in this country is based upon a fundamental approach with a small minority of investors concerned exclusively with the technical approach (covered next). In the final analysis there is no real substitute for a comprehensive understanding of a firm and a correct assessment of its prospects. The ability to uncover inside information or to accurately forecast a company's future earnings is an invaluable asset, but of questionable legality. The stream of future earnings and dividends constitutes what a stock is ultimately worth to its investors. When these earnings and dividends are estimated precisely, true value is defined. All that remains is to purchase those stocks priced beneath their true value and to sell them when they become priced in excess of that value. But few individual investors can afford to devote the time and money required for such value analyses, and those that can, find the value estimation task exceedingly difficult, if not impossible.

Hundreds of millions of dollars are spent on Wall Street each year to estimate company values, their growth potential and to formulate investment decisions. To judge from the historical portfolio experiences of those large investors (e.g., mutual funds, pension funds, bank trust departments) who have been able to devote the necessary effort to analyzing fundamentals, it must be extremely difficult to estimate true value or growth potential. Why? Because very few of these fundamentalists have been able to *consistently* derive better than average investment results, and in recent years most have underperformed the market.

There is a good reason for this. Aside from occasional leaks of inside information (which the Securities and Exchange Commission is vigorously trying to eliminate), most fundamental analysts have access to and analyze the same information. Such basic measures as: debt/equity ratios, current assets ratios, historical sales and earnings growth rates, dividend payout ratios, yields, price/earnings ratios, and the like are commonplace and overused. In most cases any predictive value they might have is incorporated into current stock prices so rapidly as to eliminate their usefulness. If any of these measures do have some residual value, it is probably only at the bullish extreme. Companies which appear to be exceptionally undervalued might be isolated for further analysis and then purchased if the undervaluation is confirmed by other factors: subjective or objective, fundamental or technical.

So what to do? Well, consider investing in an index fund or index stock. If you can't otherwise beat the average, you can meet it (and outperform most other mutual funds) by investing in a market index stock or fund. This approach will be examined under the school of efficient markets.

• **Additional comments on the worth of fundamental analysis.** Stock price changes are caused by three factors. The first is a properly recognized change in value. This, as previously noted, is within the realm of fundamental analysis but it is so difficult to measure that it may be eliminated from further consideration.

The second factor is a more or less erroneous change in investors' perceptions of value. Since value is based upon what will occur in the future (future earnings, future dividends), it would seem at first glance that with each passing moment the marketplace should logically develop a newer and keener perception of it. But in fact an infinite future always lies ahead and value always retains its basic elusiveness: it never becomes easier to estimate merely with the passage of time.

Then, there is the third factor, which may turn out to be the most important one—investors are creatures of emotion. They remember the price they paid for a stock and this can influence their decisions of when and at what price to sell it.

The School Of Technical Analysis. Technical analysis is a very broad topic because there are so many varieties of this type of analysis. In general, technical analysis attempts to predict future stock prices by analyzing past stock prices. In effect, it asserts that tomorrow's stock price is influenced by today's price. That is a very appealing assertion, because it eliminates the need to perform fundamental analysis. No longer does the investor have to be concerned with earnings, ratios, estimating growth, and appropriate discount rates. Instead, "technicalists" need only keep a record of specific market factors, such as, price changes, volume, momentum and trends.

In contrast to fundamental analysis, which is the determination of value and the purchase or sale of stocks whose price deviates from value, technical analysis is based upon two very different premises. First, that subjective estimates of value are simply too imprecise, and are thus effectively irrelevant. Second, future price fluctuations may be predicted through analysis of historical price movements, resistance and support relationships, and other factors that impact directly upon price. Technical analysis is devoted to studies of *resistance and support* for a company's stock (and to the market as a whole) and to those statistics that are related to price and volume.

For ease of presentation, I have broken down the school of technical analysis into two groups; *chartists* and *market timers.*

• **Chartists.** Chartists are primarily interested in specific information on *individual* stocks, such as, the closing price and the volume of transactions.

Chartists are guided by historical chart patterns created by the movements of the stock prices for indications of what's going to happen next. Some of these patterns are known by such picturesque names as "head and shoulders," "double tops," "triangles," "gaps," and "rising bottoms." Chartists also look for cyclical patterns in hopes of spotting relationships that appear ready to repeat themselves. This information is then summarized in a variety of forms, such as, charts and graphs, which in turn tell the chartist when to buy and sell these securities.

• **Chart types and their utilization.** The three standard types of charts are the bar, line, and point and figure. In each case the amount of information available and its intended use determine the type of chart chosen to record price activity.

• **The bar chart.** The bar chart is the most commonly used technical tool. It is simple to construct as it portrays the high, low, and closing prices of a particular stock or stock market average, for a particular time period chosen. In the latter regard, bar charts are kept either on a daily, weekly, or monthly basis. The type of bar chart will, of course, be predicated upon the time horizon of the investor.

A bar chart is illustrated in Figure 8.1. In this example, the high, low and weekly closing price of a "Large Cap Stock" fund are plotted over a three year time frame from August 1997. The figure also contains two moving averages (running through the price curve). The solid line is a 13-week moving average and the dashed line is a 39-week moving average. Notice how the 13 week moving average follows the price movement of the stock much closer than the 39 week moving average which lags the rises and drops of the actual price changes. This is because or the way the moving average is calculated. The 13-week moving average has one-third the number of terms in the average. In addition, at the bottom of the figure, there is a *relative strength* plot and a *momentum* plot denoted. These types of plots and their utility will be discussed later in this chapter.

Figure 8.1 The Bar Chart of A "Large Capitalization Stock" Fund

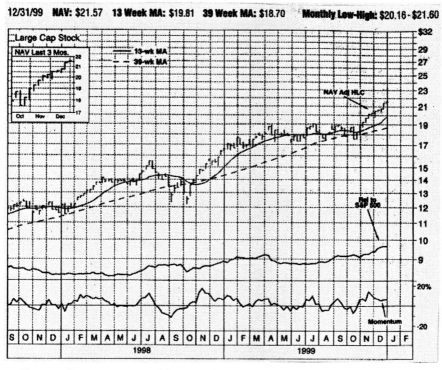

12/31/99 NAV: $21.57 13 Week MA: $19.81 39 Week MA: $18.70 Monthly Low-High: $20.16 - $21.60

(Source: "Large Cap Stock" mutual Fund, Mutual Fund Guide, Fidelity Investments. Special 1999 Year End Issue p.50)

• **Line charts.** The line chart's primary use is to denote the trend of a single statistic. As an example, the daily closing price of a stock; a weekly group statistic; or a monthly economic figure would most often be plotted on a line chart basis. For example, in Figure 8.1, if you connected all the weekly closing prices and eliminated the vertical lines that connected each week's high and low, this would be a three year weekly line chart whose group statistic would be the price trend of all large cap stock.

The two types of charting techniques reviewed above can be portrayed on graph paper utilizing one of two types of scales—the arithmetic or semi-log delineation. Again, the utilization of the type of scale depends greatly upon the desires of the chartist. There are those who wish to analyze stock price movements on a percentage basis and therefore their graphs would be kept on a semilog basis. Long-term trend analysis is often more useful on a semi-log (geometrical) price scale. On the other hand, others desire simple short-term trend analysis, or stock price movement in terms of points rather than percentages. Thus, for them, a straight arithmetic scale suffices. Later, in chapter 12, there is a bar chart plotted with a semi-log scale and an arithmetic scale for about the same time period. There are positive and negative factors for each approach, most often hinging on the price level of the stock and the amount of price history under study.

• **Point and figure charts.** To many, the point and figure approach is a bit more mysterious, and indeed to some, the mastering of the technique of maintaining a point and figure chart is a cumbersome chore. Unlike the bar chart, the basic difference in a point and figure graph is that there is no distinct depiction of volume trends.

Like the bar chart, there are a number of different types of point and figure graphs utilized—again, depending upon your time horizon or investment philosophy. Whereas, a bar chart depicts a daily, weekly, or monthly specific price range, a point and figure chart illustrates trades only as they occur, and in their sequence.

The essence of point and figure charts, which are also called X-O charts, seek to identify changes in resistance and support by watching changes in security prices. If a stock's price goes up, that movement is caused by support and the chart is constructed by putting an X on the chart (in the X-column for that day) when the price rises by an arbitrary value, such as $1 or $2. If the price remains stable there is no entry in the chart. However, if there is an *increased* shift in resistance, the price drops, and a O is entered on the chart (in the O-column for that day) to indicate a downwards price change of the $1 or $2 value.

When setting up an X-O chart, time is placed on the horizontal axis and dollars on the vertical axis. The dollar unit selected depends on the value of the stock. It is interesting that purchases and sales appear to be made at the wrong times. When an X is entered, it's after the stock has already increased in price. Conversely, when a O is entered, it's made after the stock has declined. The rationale for this behavior rests primarily in the belief that the charts indicate new trends. During an *upward* trend each high is higher than the preceding high price, and each low is also higher than the preceding low price. Obviously, if you buy this stock and hold it, the return will be positive over this period. However, the return may be increased by judiciously buying at each low, selling at each high, and repeating the process when the cycle within the trend is repeated.

As the chart progresses day after day, a set of lines can be drawn connecting the highs of each day and the lows of each day. The purpose of these lines is to isolate the buy and sell opportunities. The bottom lines suggest a price level that generates "support" for the stock; that is, this is a good time to buy the stock. Technical analysis asserts that when the price of the stock approaches a support line, the number of purchases will increase, which will stop further price declines. Hence, the approach of a stock's price toward a support level suggests that a buying opportunity is developing. Should the price reach the line and start back up, then you should buy the stock. The opposite occurs at the top line that represents a "resistance." Since the price of the stock has risen to that level, more investors will want to sell their stock, which will thwart further price advances. Accordingly, you should sell the stock when the price reaches a line of resistance. After the stock has been sold, you should wait for the price to decline at the level of price support to repeat the cycle.

• **Market timers.** Sometimes technical analysts are specifically interested in the market as a whole and use special technical methods that are designed to indicate the general direction of the market. These are called market timers. Market timers look at the market trends and volume thus creating moneymaking opportunities to determine an opportune time to buy or sell the market. There are various types of market timers that use specific approaches to determining when the market is a good time to buy and the right time to sell. There is one type of chartist that believes that if the number of stock issues rising in price exceeds the number of declining issues by a certain amount for a certain length of time, the market is headed up for a while. This "advance-decline" theory is also said to work on the downside.

Another type of market timer espouses the "Dow theory." The Dow theory, named after one of the founders of Dow Jones, is one of the most widely followed methods of technical analysis. It holds that a significant market move, up or down (a bull or bear market), is underway when a change in the primary direction of the DJIA, is confirmed by the Dow Jones Transportation index (which is composed of 20 transportation-industry stocks moving in the same direction at the same time). Disciples of the Dow theory don't claim that it will predict a change in the market direction, just that it will confirm it in time for attentive investors to take advantage of the primary trend.

There are several problems with the Dow theory. The first is that it is not a theory but an interpretation of known data. It does not explain why the two averages should be able to forecast future stock prices. In addition, there may be a considerable lag between the actual turning points and those indicated by the forecast. It may be months before the two averages confirm each other, during which time individual stocks may show substantial change.

The accuracy of the Dow theory and its predictive power has been the subject of many debates. Greiner and Whitcomb assert that "the Dow Theory provides a time-tested method of reading the stock market barometer." However, between 1929 and 1960 the Dow theory made only nine correct predictions out of 24 buy or sell signals. These results however, were not corroborated by another study that concluded that from 1971 to 1980, the theory generated returns in excess of 14 percent.

• **Stock and market trends.** You may not want to get too involved in all the possible applications of technical analysis. In fact, you may just want to use charts as nothing more than a road map of the market or a particular stock. Trend lines constitute a very important element of charting theory. Trend line analysis of price movements in a stock market chart can aid you to at least examine where on the route you will be making a commitment. Trend lines are drawn on a price chart by connecting two points. An uptrend line connects two or more interim low prices with a straight line in an upward slope. A downtrend line connects two or more price peaks in a downward direction. Depending on the duration of the chart, short, intermediate and long term, price trends can be so delineated.

Chartists like to construct channels. A channel requires two trend lines drawn parallel to each other, one on each side of the price figures plotted on the chart. A simple observation of a stock's chart channel can reveal the precise point in trend when an alert for a trading commitment should be made. According to trend analysis theory, a stock is expected to remain within its channel, if not it becomes a "breakout"—to the upside (a bullish indicator) and to the downside (a bearish indicator).

• **The psychology behind stock market trends.** As simple as it is, a trendline can be a powerful technical tool to the novice and professional alike. "The trend is your friend," is the positive cliché to the old "Don't fight the trend" slogan. Trendlines give guidance to the short-term trader and the longer-term investor. The trader can use trend progressions for the establishment of a "stop-loss" order while the investor can "let their profits run" using the elementary trendline approach. Trendlines can also keep the "bottom fisher" from entering too early and getting caught in the final declining phase—the "blowoff"—of the stock's free-fall. A stock can't go up until it stops going down, and the breaking of down trendlines will be the first clue that negative momentum is waning.

Stock (and market) trends often tend to accelerate at or near the end of a move. On the upside, the acceleration of support can be likened to the "everyone's got to own 'em" stage. On the downside, the familiar climactic "washout" occurs. These respective trends some investors refer to as the greed and fear stages.

• **Supply and demand forces at work.** The mere violation of a trendline is not the sole reason a technical analyst becomes concerned. It's the implied change in the resistance or support trend lines behind the shift that is meaningful. An uptrend, by definition, is a series of higher lows followed by higher highs, in that sequence. A downtrend is, of course, the opposite progression. Staying with the uptrend, let's more fully define the higher low, higher high progression in terms of resistance and support terms. Who creates the higher low? The higher high?

It is simple logic that a buyer (demand) is the force creating the higher lows in an uptrend. And the persistence of support (demand), over time, is what creates the higher low pattern. On the resistance side, the seller (supply) is actually profiling a bullish bent. How? Because the seller is selling at progressively higher levels. So, an uptrend is not just a series of higher lows and higher highs but actually the portrayal, over time, of the supply-demand forces at work. Therefore, they are bullish signs of support (demand for the stock—buyers) and resistance (suppliers of the stock—sellers). Once these forces begin to change their style (for whatever reason), the technical analyst will be alerted by trend violations. Uptrend violations will most often be spotted by the support factor first giving a clue of change. The higher lows will not follow through. Then the technical analyst will look for signs of a change in the resistance side, which will manifest itself by a change in the progression of the higher highs. Lower highs, followed by lower lows, will be the complete evidence of a trend change from positive to negative.

We try to remember that stocks often look "expensive" in bull markets, yet they can continue to climb. Stocks often look "cheap" in major bear trends, and they can get "cheaper." Trend analysis, while very simple from a supply-demand view of the market, provides an important discipline for "letting profits run," and "cutting losses short."

• **Relative strength.** One of the oldest approaches of technical analysis, and still one of the most widely used is relative strength. As the term signifies, action of a stock or a group of stocks is often compared to the market as a whole, so that it can be determined whether or not the stock is acting better than or worse than the market.

Making money in a bull market is not a difficult task. If the general trend is up, you would have much better than a 50 percent chance that a "dart" thrown at the stock table would result in the "choice" of a winner. In these days of competitive performance on the professional level, relative performance has taken on an even more important aspect. Professional portfolio managers must show the ability to outperform the market or else funds can be invested in an "index fund" that is guaranteed to emulate the market with little or no management fee. Such "passive" portfolio management has grown extensively in recent years for at least a portion of pension assets.

Technicians often apply relative strength analysis first to the market's groups, believing that a strong group is a prerequisite to picking a strong stock. Academic research supports this view. There is an old cliché "that a rising tide lifts all boats." While you can pick a good-acting stock from a broad relative strength stock screen, it's a lot easier if the tide of the group's behavior is rising.

Many different mathematical computations may be used to calculate relative strength, but the simplest (and most common) is when the daily (or weekly) close of a stock (or group) is divided by a market average or index, most often the S&P 500. The result can be related to a specific time period to result in a ratio. If this ratio moves up or down over a period of time, it will indicate whether or not the stock is acting better than or worse than the general market trend. A stock that is moving laterally while the market is trending lower will possess a strong relative strength curve. A stock that is moving laterally as the market moves laterally will possess flat relative strength, indicating that the issue is acting in line with the general market trend.

Many times the technical analyst will use relative strength to determine future market leadership, or the pending loss of same. Groups that act well in the tail end of a bear market, often emerge as the new bull market's leaders. Leaders in a bull market may show signs of losing that status if relative strength "divergence" begins to profile a mature trend. Simply said, if the absolute price index of a group goes on to make a bull trend high without the relative numbers confirming, a change in the group's trend may not be far off.

Comments On The Worth Of Technical Analysis. Technical analysis is the art of identifying patterns from a chart of the price movement of a particular security or market. Technical analysts believe that profits above the market's overall rate of return can be earned by predicting future price movements based on past patterns. But the past isn't necessarily prologue and history rarely repeats itself exactly. Investors who use a market timing approach exclusively have about the same record of beating the averages as other professionals. Nonetheless, the investor who doesn't make a point of becoming familiar with them is missing out on an opportunity to enhance returns.

Investors tend to allow themselves to be caught up in the market atmosphere of the moment, be it greed, panic, fear, or even apathy. All those fundamentalists looking at the same factors at the same time tend to move prices to extremes. Thus prices tend to move in trends, and trend following (one of the basic precepts of technical analysis), has a valid theoretical basis. One reason for great sustained bull market trends is doubtless the plethora of optimistic earnings reports which emerge after an economic upswing is well in progress. Investors tend to jump aboard those issues exhibiting the greatest "fundamental" improvement and bid them up to greater extremes. Such situations offer profit opportunities to technicians trading with prevailing price trends. At the same time they ultimately spell doom, both for the fundamentalists who bought stocks at the high and for the not inconsiderable number of technicians who bought earlier for purely technical reasons but then "fell in love" with the fundamentals at the peak. (The true technical analyst throws in the towel when prices begin to fall. Fundamentalists, on the other hand, just think stocks are cheaper and are therefore better buys than ever.) By the time the fundamental news turns sour and the reasons for the decline are widely understood, the process is usually ready to reverse itself. A similar situation, then, works during bear markets as well. Thus, technical indicators are frequently useful in the timing process. There is indeed an abundance of technical stock selection systems. Of course, not all of them work all of the time. (Some, frankly, don't work at all.)

• **Selection strategies.** A caveat worth remembering at this point is that *something* always works best. Unfortunately, computers make it easy to test everything and find the something that worked best in the past. But, if what works best doesn't have a sound theoretical and practical basis, it is probably meaningless.

Another very important consideration is that different market environments dictate different stock selection strategies. For example, the purchase of stocks priced far below book value per share was very profitable in the 1940s and 1950s. But during the soaring '60s such systems became relatively unprofitable and new issues, conglomerates and glamour stocks caught on. Relative strength analysis also has its place, but it is a useful tool only during certain phases of the market cycle.

The School Of Efficient Markets.
Economics teaches that financial markets with many participants, i.e., buyers and sellers who can enter and exit freely, will be competitive. In a free and open marketplace virtually anyone may purchase and sell stocks and bonds. In this country, many firms,

including banks, insurance companies and mutual funds, compete for investors' funds. Our financial markets are perhaps the most competitive of all markets in the world. In addition to expecting a return on their investment, investors also bear risks, that is, the possibility of loss or the uncertainty of returns.

• **Why financial markets tend to be very efficient.** Security prices depend on future cash flows, such as, interest or dividend payments. If new information suggests that these flows will be altered, the market rapidly adjusts the security's price. Thus, an efficient financial market implies that a security's current price embodies all the known information concerning the potential return and risk associated with the particular security. If a stock were undervalued and offered an excessive return, investors would seek to buy it, which would drive the price up and reduce the return that subsequent investors would earn. Conversely, if the stock were overvalued and offered an inferior return, investors would seek to sell it, which would drive its price down and decrease the return to subsequent investors. The fact that there are sufficient "informed" investors means that a stock's price will reflect the investment community's consensus regarding it's true value and that the expected return will be consistent with the amount of risk the investor must bear to earn that return.

• **Axiom 1. You can't beat the market consistently.** The concept of an efficient financial market has an important and sobering consequence. Efficient markets indicate that investors (or at least the vast majority of investors) cannot expect, on the average, to beat the market *consistently*. Of course, that does not mean an individual will never select a stock that does exceedingly well. Individuals can earn large returns on particular stocks, as the stockholders of many companies know. What the concept of efficient markets implies is that you cannot consistently select those individual companies that earn abnormally large returns.

The converse is also true. If you cannot expect to outperform the market consistently, you should not expect to consistently underperform the market either. Of course, some stocks may decline in price and inflict large losses to your portfolio, but efficient markets imply that you will not always select the stocks of companies that fail. If you were so unfortunate, you will soon lose your money and will no longer be able to participate in the stock market.

The bottom line of efficient-market theory implies that you should, over an extended period of time, earn neither excessively positive nor excessively negative returns. Instead your returns should mirror the returns earned by the stock market as a whole and the risk that you are willing to bear. Although security prices and returns are ultimately determined by the interactions of buyers and sellers, there really is very little that you can do to affect a stock's price. Instead, you should select among the various alternatives to build a portfolio that is consistent with your financial goals and the risk level you're willing to bear.

The Theory Behind Efficient-Markets. There are some individuals who boast that they can use a valuation model, or P/E ratios, or some other technique to outperform the market on a risk-adjusted basis. Notice the use of the phrase "risk-adjusted basis." Bearing more risk implies the individual should earn a higher return than the market. To outperform the market and earn an excess return, the investor must do better than the return that would be expected given the amount of risk.

As previously stated, the adherents of the efficient-market theory, investors cannot expect to *outperform the market consistently* on a risk-adjusted basis over an extended period of time. Being an occasional winner is not what is important to the efficient-market theory followers. Being a consistent winner is, because that would be an anomaly. Anomalies will be discussed in depth later in this chapter.

• **What's in a name, "random walk" or efficient-market theory.** Academicians have to continue to publish to maintain their position or rank in the university environment. One way to do this is to rename something existing by a new catchy name, such as, calling the efficient-market theory the *random walk theory*. The random walk theory is based on the same premises as the efficient-market theory, that 1) security prices reflect all available information concerning a company, and 2) security prices change very rapidly in response to new information. As we have seen, security prices fully incorporate known information and prices change rapidly; academicians say that these changes will follow in a "random walk" over time. The random walk term implies that price "changes" are unpredictable and *patterns* formed in line charts, bar charts, or in point and figure charts are accidental. If prices do follow a random walk, trading rules are useless, and various techniques, such as, fundamental analysis, technical analysis, moving averages, or any other strategic strategy cannot lead to superior security selection.

The choice of the term "random walk" by academicians to describe the pattern of changes in security prices is unfortunate for two reasons. First, it is reasonable to expect that over a period of time, stock prices will rise. Unless the stock return is entirely the result of dividends, stock prices must rise to generate a positive return. In addition, historically, stock prices tend to rise over time as companies and the economy grow.

Second, the phrase "random walk" is often misinterpreted as meaning that security values, e.g., stock prices are randomly determined, an interpretation that is totally incorrect. Actually, it is the *time of occurrence* or "when" the price change occurs that is random. Stock prices themselves are rationally and efficiently determined by such fundamental considerations as earnings, interest rates, dividend policy, industry type and the economic environment. Changes in theses variables are quickly reflected in a stock's price. All known information is embodied in the current price, and only new information will alter that price. New information has to be unpredictable; if it were predictable, the information would be known and stock prices would have already adjusted for that information. Hence, new information must be random, and stock prices should change randomly in response to that information. If changes in stock prices were not random and could be predicted, then some investors could consistently outperform the market, that is, earn a return in excess of the expected return given the amount of risk, and security markets would not be efficient.

• **The stock price is always right.** Since the efficient-market theory maintains that the current price of a stock properly values the company's future growth and dividends, then today's price is a true measure of the stock's worth. However, according to the school of fundamental analysis, that analysis is designed to determine if the stock is over- or underpriced; but, the efficient-market theory states that this effort is futile because the stock is neither. If prices were not true measures of the company's worth, an opportunity to earn excess returns would exist. Investors would recognize these opportunities and take advantage of the mispricing and would consistently outperform the market on a risk-adjusted basis by purchasing undervalued stock or shorting overvalued stock.

Academicians have established the efficient-market theory as the cornerstone for all modern financial investment courses taught in today's business schools. You just cannot pass basic finance 101, receive your MBA degree, obtain a license as a stock broker, or be certified as a financial planner (CFP) or financial analyst (CFA) unless you give credence to the efficient-market theory. Well, perhaps you don't have to swear to the credibility of the theory but you do have to pass the final examination using it's concepts.

• **The rapidity of price adjustments.** For security markets to be efficient, security prices must adjust rapidly. The efficient-market theory asserts that the market prices adjust rapidly as new information is disseminated. In the electronic world of the internet, cell phones, 24 hour availability of stock market results on television, financial information is instantaneously disbursed to the investment community. The market then adjusts security prices in accordance with the impact of the news on the company's future earnings and dividends. By the time the individual investor learns of the information, security prices probably will have already changed. Thus, the investor will not be able to profit from acting on the information.

If the market data were not so efficient and prices did not adjust almost instantaneously, some investors would be able to adjust their holdings and take advantage of differences in investors' knowledge. Consider the example of an expected merger of two companies that had abruptly terminated. If some investors knew that the agreement had been terminated but others did not, the former could sell their holdings to those who were not informed. The price then may fall over a period of time as the knowledgeable sellers accepted progressively lower prices in order to unload their stock. Of course, if a sufficient number of investors had learned quickly of the termination, the price decline would have been a "free-fall" as these investors dumped their stock in accordance with the new information. If an investor were able to anticipate the termination of the merger before it was announced, that individual could avoid the free-fall. Every year, there are cases where some investors sell their shares just prior to an announcement, but it is also evident that some individuals bought those shares.

Versions Of The Financial Market's Efficiency. The competition among investors, the rapid dissemination of information, and the speed with which security prices adjust to this information produce efficient financial markets in which an investor cannot expect to consistently out-perform the market. Instead, investors can expect to earn a return that is consistent with the amount of risk they bear.

While the financial academicians agreed that financial markets were efficient, they were not quite sure how efficient. The degree of efficiency is important, because it determines the value the individual investor places on various types of analysis to select securities. Academicians responded by establishing three versions of the random walk, or efficient-market theory. These versions, or *forms*, are the "weak," the "semi-strong," and the "strong" form. All embrace the general belief that—except for the long term trends where the stock market will advance—future stock prices are impossible to predict.

• **The "first" degree of efficiency—the "Weak" form.** The weak form attacks the underpinnings of technical analysis; it says you cannot predict future stock prices on the basis of past stock prices. Studying past price behavior, patterns and other technical indicators of the market will not produce superior investment results. Technical indicators do not produce returns on securities that are in excess of the return that is consistent with the amount of risk borne by the investor.

• **The "second" degree of efficiency—the "Semi-strong" form.** The semi-strong and strong form argue against many of the beliefs held by those using fundamental analysis. The semi-strong form asserts that the current price of a stock reflects all of the public's information concerning the company. This knowledge includes both the company's past history and the information learned through studying a company's financial statements, its industry, and the general economic environment. Analysis of this data cannot be *expected* to produce superior results. The implication here is that even if fundamental analysis produces superior results in some cases, it will not produce superior results over many investment decisions.

By far the most research and the most interest lies with the semi-strong form of the efficient-market theory. Studies of strategies that use publicly available information such as the data found in a company's financial statements have generally concluded that this information does not produce superior results. Prices change very rapidly once information becomes public, and thus, the security's price embodies all known information. If an investor could anticipate the new information, e.g., the "whisper number" of a firm's expected earnings, and act before the information became public, that individual might be able to outperform the market, but once the information becomes public, it rarely can be used to generate superior investment results.

• **The "third" degree of efficiency—the "Strong" form.** The strong form frankly states that nothing—not even "unpublished" developments—can be of use in predicting future prices; everything known, or even knowable, has already been reflected in present prices. Thus, not even access to inside information can be expected to result in superior investment performance. Once again, the implication here is that even if an individual acts on inside information which, in some cases produces superior results, that these results cannot be expected and that success in one case will tend to be offset by failure in other cases. So, over time, the investor will not achieve superior results.

This conclusion rests on a very important assumption: Inside information cannot be kept inside! Too many people know about the activities of a company. Of course, most investors do not have access to inside information or at least do not have access to information concerning a number of companies. An individual may have access to privileged information concerning a company for which they work. But, the use of such information for personal gain is illegal. To achieve continuous superior results, the individual would have to have a continuous supply of correct inside information and to use it illegally. Probably few, if any, investors have this continuous supply, which may explain why both fundamental and technical analysts watch sales and purchases by insiders as a means to glean a clue as to the "true" future potential of the company as seen by its management.

Knowledge of this inefficiency, however, may have led to its demise, in other words, the inefficiency corrected itself. Insiders must register their trading activity with the SEC. Since the SEC publishes an Official Summary of Insider Trading, non-insiders can track purchases and sales by insiders and act accordingly. Once individuals start to follow such a strategy, the inefficiency may disappear. One study found that a strategy of buying after insider purchases and selling after insider sales failed to produce a return that was large enough to overcome the commissions associated with the trading strategy. Thus, unless the investor had minimal transaction costs (a few large mutual funds may have sufficiently small transaction costs), the strategy did not produce excess returns. This result supports the strong form of the efficient-market theory.

The Anomalies Of The Efficient-market Theory. While the evidence generally supports market efficiency, academia has established the three forms to explain away the degrees of efficiency. This raises an interesting question. If the financial markets are not completely efficient what are the exceptions? This question has led to the identification of exceptions referred to as *anomalies*. A market anomaly is a situation or strategy that cannot be explained away but would *not be expected* to happen if the efficient-market theory were completely true. For example, if buying shares in companies that announced a stock split led to excess returns, such a strategy would imply that security markets are not entirely efficient.

In his book on investments, H.B. Mayo references papers and studies that identify six anomalies of the efficient-market theory. They are the, 1) "P/E effect," 2) "small-firm effect," 3) "January effect," 4) "neglected firm effect," 5) "day of the week effect," and 6) "Value Line ranking system effect."

• **The "P/E effect."** This effect indicates that portfolios consisting of stocks with low price-earnings ratios have a higher average return than portfolios with higher P/E ratios.

• **The "small-firm effect."** This effect, also known as the *small-cap effect* for small capitalization companies, suggests that returns diminish as the size of the company rises. Size is generally measured by the firm's market value, i.e., the product of the stock outstanding and it's net asset value. If all common stocks on the New York Stock Exchange are divided into five groups, the smallest quintile (the smallest 20 percent of the total companies) has tended to earn a return that exceeds the return on investments in the stocks that comprise the largest quintile, even after adjusting for risk.

• The "**January effect.**" Subsequent studies have found that the small-firm effect occurs primarily in January, especially the first five trading days. This anomaly is referred to as the "January effect. The January effect is often explained by the fact that investors buy-back stocks in January after selling for income-tax reasons in December. And there is some evidence that within a size class those stocks whose prices declined the most in the preceding year tended to rebound the most during January.

• The "**neglected-firm effect.**" This effect suggests that small companies which are neglected by large financial institutions tend to generate higher returns than those companies favored by financial institutions. By dividing companies into the categories of highly researched stocks, moderately researched stocks, and neglected stocks (based on the number of institutions holding the stock), researchers have found that the last group outperformed the more well-researched companies. This anomaly is probably another variation of the small-firm effect, that the market gets less efficient as companies get smaller. Since large financial institutions may exclude these companies from consideration, their lack of participation reduces the market's efficiency.

• The "**day-of-the-week effect.**" Presumably there is no reason to anticipate that day-to-day returns should differ except over the weekend when the return should exceed the return earned from one weekday to the next. However, research has suggested that the weekend does not generate a higher return but a lower return. If this anomaly is true, it implies that investors anticipating the purchase of stock should not buy on Friday but wait until Monday. Investors anticipating the sale of stock should reverse the procedure. If this anomaly is true, it should be erased by investors selling short on Friday and covering their positions on Monday (i.e., an act of arbitrage should erase the anomaly). The existence of the anomaly is generally resolved by asserting that the excess return is too small to cover transaction costs.

• **The "*Value Line Investment Survey* effect.**" *Value Line* ranks all the stocks that it covers weekly into five groups ranging from those most likely to outperform the market during the next twelve months (i.e., stocks ranked "1") to those that are likely to underperform the market during the next twelve months (stocks 'ranked "5"'). Several studies have found that using the Value Line ranking system, i.e., selecting stocks ranked "1") generates an excess return, hence the "Value Line effect." Once again, the smaller companies tended to generate the largest excess return. While the amount of this excess return differed among the various studies, its existence is inconsistent with the efficient-market theory. However, it may be exceedingly difficult for the individual investor to take advantage of the anomaly since the Value Line rankings change weekly, which will require substantial transaction costs as investors frequently adjusts their portfolio.

While most evidence supports the efficient-market theory, the conclusion indicates that there appear to be exceptions. Perhaps the observed exceptions are the result of flaws in the research methodology. Furthermore, any evidence supporting a particular inefficiency cannot be used to support other possible inefficiencies; it applies only to the specific anomaly under study.

Caveats On Using The Efficient-Market Theory Anomalies. Before you rush out to take advantage of these alleged inefficiencies, Mayo reminds us of five sobering considerations. "First, the empirical results are only consistent with inefficiencies; they do not prove their existence. Second, for the investor to take advantage of the inefficiency, it must be ongoing. Once an inefficiency is discovered and investors seek to take advantage of it, the inefficiency will probably disappear. Third, transaction costs are important, and the investor must pay the transaction costs associated with the strategy. Fourth, the investor still must select individual issues. Even if small companies outperform the market in the first week of January, the individual investor cannot purchase all of them. There is no assurance that the selected stocks will be those that outperform the market in that particular year. Fifth, for an anomaly to be useful for an active investment strategy, its signals must be transferable to the individual investor. Just because the Value Line rankings produce excess returns in an empirical study does not mean that the individual investor may be able to receive the information rapidly enough to act upon it. The anomaly may exist for those investors with the first access to the information, but not to all investors who receive the recommendations."

The Utility Of The Efficient-Market Theory. Ultimately, you must decide for yourself the degree of efficiency and whether the anomalies are grounds for particular strategies. If you have a proclivity toward active investment management you may see these anomalies as an opportunity. If you prefer more passive investment management you may see them as nothing more than interesting curiosities.

• **The first utility.** An efficient market implies that investors and financial analysts are using known information to correctly value what a security is worth. You may not be able to use public information to achieve superior investment results because the investment community is already using and acting on that information. It is this very fact that investors as a group are competent and are trying to beat each other that helps to produce efficient markets.

• **The second utility.** The efficient-market theory applies to an individual's portfolio. The efficient-market theory indicates that you could randomly select a diversified portfolio of securities and earn a return consistent with the market as a whole. Furthermore, once the portfolio has been selected, there is no need to change it. This "buy-and-hold-forever" strategy has the additional advantage of minimizing commissions. The problem with this strategic investment technique is that it fails to consider the reasons an investor saves and acquires stock and other assets. The goals behind the portfolio are disregarded, and different goals require different portfolio construction strategies. Furthermore, goals and conditions change with time, which in turn requires changes in your portfolio. When your goals or financial situation change, the portfolio should be altered in a way that is consistent with the new goals and conditions.

• **The third utility.** The importance of the efficient-market theory to the individual investor is not the implication that investment decision making is useless. Instead, it brings to the foreground the environment in which you must make decisions. The theory should make you realize that investments in securities may not produce superior returns. Rather, you should earn a return over a period of time that is consistent with the return earned by the market as a whole and the amount of risk borne by you. This means that you should devote more time and effort to the selection of your investment goals and the type of securities to meet those goals than to the analysis of individual securities. Since such analysis cannot be expected to produce superior returns, it takes resources and time away from the important questions of why you save and invest.

The Worth Of The Efficient-market Theory. The efficient-market theory can be condensed into five axioms:

• **Axiom (1)** Investors cannot expect to outperform the market *consistently* on a "risk-adjusted" basis. (Bearing *less* risk implies that the investor should earn a lower return than the market. The converse is also true.)

• **Axiom (2)** For security prices to be efficient, security prices must adjust rapidly.

• **Axiom (3)** Since security prices, in rapid response to new information, reflect all available information concerning the company's stock, price changes are unpredictable and patterns formed are accidental. Thus, the next move in a series of stock prices is unpredictable on the basis of past price behavior.

• **Axiom (4)** Trading rules are useless, and various techniques, e.g., charting, moving averages or other advertised techniques cannot lead to superior security selection or outperform the market consistently.

• **Axiom** (5) The current price of a stock efficiently values the company's *future* growth and dividends. (Stock prices themselves are rationally and efficiently determined by the "five pillars of the market"—dividend policy, earnings, interest rate, inflation rate, and the company's valuation—price-to-earnings ratio).

Conclusions. Normally, it would be unfair and misleading to assert that any one stock selection system or portfolio management strategy is always the right one or the wrong one. The efficient-market theory notwithstanding, this book is predicated on a unique technical approach that supplements the efficient-market theory. The theory establishes the generally accepted baseline for the stock market investment strategy. In the next chapter, I will present another approach to stock market investing which, if proven accurate, is the seventh anomaly to the six efficient-market theory anomalies already documented. The anomaly is called the "Y-Process anomaly" or for short the "Y-Process".

9

The Y-Process: A Stock Market Strategy
For Sophisticated Investors

THE Y-PROCESS USES A MARKET MODEL THAT FORECASTS CRUCIAL MARKET TURNS ENABLING THE INVESTOR TO REDUCE RISK AND ENHANCE RETURNS.

Stock Market Forecasting. One of the fundamental tools of the physical scientist is mathematics. Mathematics is the means by which physicists and chemists can describe the motions and interactions of atoms and molecules. Social sciences, such as psychology and sociology, involve so many parameters that mathematical equations are not very useful to describe or predict the behavior of people or groups. Since forecasting stock market turns is in the same category as the social sciences, to be successful, one would have to predict the behavior of investors.

The Y-Process' model is founded on two quintessential market concepts, (1) the law of supply and demand, and (2) that stock prices tend to move in trends. For the stock market dynamics of supply and demand to function effectively requires an efficient and competitive market place where buyers and sellers meet in an auction process. In this market place, there is a buyer for every seller of stocks. But one of these forces is usually more influential—since the market is a "discounting mechanism." This means that events, which affect a stock's price, are usually discounted in advance with movements that are the result of "informed" buyers and sellers at work. It is because of this supply and demand behavior that *price forma-tions* evolve due to the convictions of all the types of investors,—funda-mentalists, speculators, technicians, "buy-and-hold-and-prayers"—putting their money to work based upon their established convictions.

• **The trend is your friend.** There is a saying that is often heard on Wall Street: "The trend is your friend." The Y-Process is a model that synthe-size the precursors of change in the market's trend, i.e., whether a bull market or bear market is in process. The Y-Process' greatest feature is its ability to detect the transition from bull to bear, or from bear to bull, very close to these major cyclical turning points.

There are two factors used in determining this transition: The market's *trend* and *moving average*. Technical analysts use trend analysis of stock price movements to aid investors to examine the market's direction and to determine the time when the market changed direction. For example, the S&P 500 Composite Stock Index's trend for the decade from 1989 through 1998 is illustrated in Figure 9.1. This decade, the most bullish in stock market history, depicts the market's continual uptrend with some zigs and zags along the way. On January 1, 1989 the S&P 500 was 280 points; it closed at 1,229 on December 31, 1998—an outstanding growth of 339%. This growth rate calculates to a 15.9% annualized return for those 10-years—the equivalent of doubling your investment every four-and-a-third years.

An observation of the market's upward trend shows that two major downturns occurred, one in 1990 and the other in 1998. The 1990 free fall (from 367 to 315) was about a 14% drop, but did not qualify as a bear market—only a *correction*. Bears require a loss of 20% or more. The 1990 downdraft (from 1187 to 974) was a shorter duration but a greater loss—about 18%—qualifying as a *severe correction* (losses of 15% or more).

• **Reading market trendline charts.** Reading the numbers of Figure 9.1 can be deceiving. The years are plotted on the horizontal axis using a linear scale (equally spaced), but, on the vertical axis, the prices are plotted nonlinearly (not equally spaced). The primary reason for this approach is to compress the data into a small space. However, there is an advantage for the investor. A one-inch vertical rise at the low S&P numbers has the same *percentage* gain as a one-inch vertical rise at the high numbers. This provides the investor the ability to easily compare price gains on a percentage basis. For example, from January 1 to May 1989, a 40-point price rise (280 to 320) is a 14.3% gain; this is one half-inch vertical rise. Ten years later, when the S&P 500 is at 1075, a one half inch vertical rise is also 14.3% gain but the point gain is almost four times greater, 153 points (1075 to 1229).

Figure 9.1   **(1989 - 1998) S&P 500 Composite Index With 3 and 9-Month Moving Averages.**

The moving average "speed" of the 3-month is much greater than the 9-month and therefore follows the Index much closer.

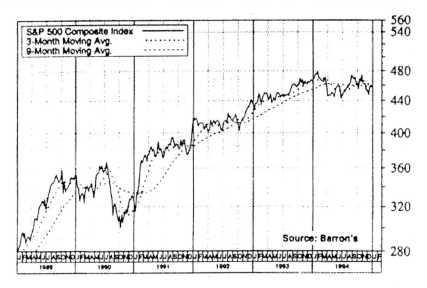

Figure 9.1   **(continued)**

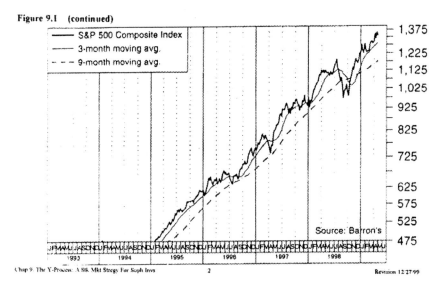

Trend Following Moving Averages. Also displayed in the figure are "3- and 9-month moving averages." A moving average is really a *mathematical trendline*. The primary purpose of a moving average (a process used in statistical mathematics) is to smooth out the numbers of the data points in order to modify minor and irregular fluctuations.

Moving averages can be created using any number of days, weeks or months. The time duration chosen affects the moving average *speed*. Moving averages can be calculated using different time periods, such as, a 10-day moving average for the short term, a 65-day moving average for the intermediate term or a 200-day moving average for the long term. The greater the number of time periods that are used the more sluggish the moving average becomes. Thus, a 13-month average is much faster (closer to the actual number) than the more sluggish 39-month moving average.

Moving averages for the same total time duration can be calculated using different time lengths as well. For example, a three-month moving average can be calculated using either a 65-day or a 13-week time length. Both are equal to three (stock market) months since the market is open only five-day week. Similarly, a nine-month moving average can be calculated using either a 200-day or a 39-week time length. In both of these cases the smaller the number of days or weeks the greater the speed or greater the tracking accuracy.

• **Moving average systems.** The array of moving average systems is almost unlimited. Some are based on moving average's rising or falling; others, on the relationships between two, three or more moving averages of different lengths, e.g., daily, weekly, monthly and the multi-dimensional array of all possibilities. To make matters even more complex, there are many types of moving averages and various techniques for calculating them.

All moving averages can be categorized into three basic types: *simple, weighted, and exponential.* A simple moving average is calculated merely by adding the closing prices of the number of days under question and dividing by the number of days. For example, a 200-day moving average would be the sum of the closes for the previous 200 market days divided by 200. This simple moving average treats all the entries equally.

The weighted and exponential moving averages place more emphasis on the more recent price activity. Many market students use the weighted or exponential varieties, because they believe that the more recent price action is more important than the price of 25, 50 or 200 days ago.

The 3- and 9-month moving averages presented in Figure 9.1 are the simple type. The 9-month moving average consists of successive averages of its 39 most recent week's closing number. Just add up the latest 39 prices and divide the total by 39. With each subsequent week, the newest closing number is incorporated into the average and the oldest 39-week's number is dropped so that the 39 most recent periods are always measured and all others are excluded. In your review of the Figure 9.1 note the speed of the 3-month moving average is much greater than the 9-month.

• **Stock market forecasting using the moving average trendline.** Although moving averages are primarily used for smoothing out irregularities in a series of market numbers, they can also be useful as the basis to formulate a stock market (or stock portfolio) forecasting system. Trading with moving averages, as the Y-Process does, will never position the investor in the market at precisely the correct time because, by its very makeup, a moving average lags the numbers they track.

A close examination of Figure 9.1 indicates that when the moving average trendline is penetrated by the index, the market trend changes direction in both the intermediate-and long-term. For example, in July and August 1990, both 3- and 9-month moving averages were penetrated on the downside, and again were penetrated on the upside in November 1990 and January 1991 respectively. Notice that in both cases, these penetrations occurred after the peak or valley had been reached and that the speedier the moving average the earlier the penetration. Notice how long it took the S&P 500 Index to get back to the previous peak in July 1990, about seven months.

Had you sold the S&P 500 Index when the 3-month moving average trendline was violated on the downside and bought it back when it was penetrated on the upside, you would have had an 11% "opportunity cost." Opportunity cost is an expression that compares current returns on a fixed number of dollars. In this case, you would take a known decrease in potential returns in exchange for unknown savings from potential losses.

One of the conditions of using moving averages in market trading is the risk of whipsaws (false trades). Whipsaws are directly correlated to the speed of the moving average, that is, the greater the speed, the greater the potential of whipsaws. On the other hand, the speedier the moving average, the smaller the "opportunity cost" on the downside and the greater the gain on the upside. The limitations of whipsaws in the Y-Process will be amplified in the next chapter.

The Searching For The Optimum Y-Process Number. The *simple* moving average is subject to criticism on two counts. First, it assigns equal weight to each of its numbers. It seems logical that recent numbers are more relevant and are more important in the average. Second, as the moving average moves through time, its *fluctuations* are dependent only on two numbers, the one being added and the one being dropped. Moving average systems that reduce these adverse effects are *weighted* or *exponential* moving average systems. Weighted or exponential systems are based on the assignment of greater weight to more recent observations and lesser weight to older numbers.

The weighted moving average is really simple to calculate, but time consuming. For a 10-day weighted moving average, you would take the current day's number and multiply it by 10, the day before times 9, the day before times 8, and so on. The final number is then divided by the sum of the multipliers for the 10-day period, which would be xxx divided by 55.

The exponential moving average which is akin to the weighted version, is even more simple to calculate in that only two numbers are used in a daily calculation, toady's price and the prior day's exponential moving average. A "smoothing constant" is first determined to use in each day's calculation. Simply defined, divide the number 2 by 1 plus the number of days you wish to smooth. For example, in a 10-day exponential moving average—2 is divided by 10 + 1 (11), this equals 0.18 which is the smoothing constant. The constant is multiplied by each day's closing price of the stock minus the prior day's exponential moving average, and then added to the prior day's exponential moving average to result in the new exponential moving average.

• **The results of the search.** To determine the optimum weighted or exponential moving average system for the Y-Process required an extensive search. Just the number of combinations and permutations of variants of time duration (speed) and the weight assigned to each observation was overwhelming

I believe that search for the optimum Y-Process number would have failed, had it not been two technologies. First, the high-speed computers which were affordable and had a mammoth storage capability. Second, modern, highly capable, computer processing technology made it possible to develop a computer program to automatically search the various combinations and permutations of the many moving average systems and "speed" for the optimum value.

The results: An exponential moving average system and a 16-week moving average speed. The baseline portfolio used for the search was the S&P 500 composite-stock index. This index was chosen because its database was extensive and available, and it is the preferred stock market benchmark of market professionals. I selected the index's closing price each Friday as the "marker" (data point) for the Y-Process number.

• **What's unique about the Y-Process number?** The Y-Process number is unique because all other moving average numbers lag the market; the

Y-Process number leads the market. In addition, the Y-Process number is a unique *moving average trendline* because it forecasts a potential bear market. If the S&P 500 index violates the Y-Process number on the downside this forecasts the possibility of a bear market. On the other hand, if the S&P 500 index penetrates the Y-Process number to the upside, this forecasts a positive change in the market's trend—from one being a negative market to the possibility of a bull market.

• **What is meant by the market cycle?** In down trending markets, it's fortunate for Y-Process users that before you suffer the onslaughts of a bear market; the market must go through three stages before it can be declared a "bear market." The first stage is a "routine" decline—a loss of 5 percent or more. Next is a "moderate correction"—a loss of 10 percent or more; this is followed by a "severe correction"—a loss of 15 percent or more. The final stage is defined as a bear market—a loss of 20 percent or more in the value of the stock market from its previous peak.

What happens after the bear market has run its course? Once the bear is exhausted, it retrenches—ultimately the index rises until the Y-Process number is penetrated to the upside which signals a new positive market trend. Simply put, once the market price rises above and remains above the Y-Process number, you should take an aggressive position by buying shares of Spiders. This step is called "going long the market." With an upside penetration, the market starts retracing its steps, backing and filling on the way up, until it exceeds its previous market high value, signaling a new bull market phase. This upward moving momentum could take a few weeks or years before the market reaches and exceeds its previous market high.

• **The simplicity of the Y-Process equations.** In addition to the Y-Process number (Y_1) there is an additional number that would be of interest to Y-Process users, that is, the number that tells you how far away you are from the dreaded bear market onslaught. This second number is called the risk index (or R). The risk index is defined as the percentage drop that the market would have to go through before it violates the Y-Process number on the downside. The results of the Y-Process derivation are provided in Equations 9.1 and 9.2.

Equation 9.1) $Y_1 = P * C_1 + Y_2 * C_2$

Equation 9.2) $R = [(P—Y_1) * C_3] \div P$

Where: $C_1 = .1177$ (smoothing constant) $Y_1 =$ the Y-Process number for next week

$C_2 = .8823$ (a constant) $Y_2 =$ last week's Y-Process number

$C_3 = 100$ (a constant) $R =$ next week's risk index (expressed in percent)

Moving average speed = 16 weeks $P =$ this week's closing price (Friday)

The Y-Process at work. An example of implementing the Y-Process is provided here by assuming an investment in the S&P 500 index from July 3, 1998 through May 21, 1999. Table 9.1 contains each week's closing S&P 500 index number. During this eight-month period, the market had a downturn that began during the middle of July. This downturn turned into a "severe correction" in the beginning of September. Cross reference Figure 9.1 again and compare it to the actual numbers in Table 9.1 which uses the Equations 9.1 and 9.2 to calculate next week's Y-Process number (Y_1) and next week's risk index (R).

Scan down the risk index column. A change from a positive number to a negative one indicates that the market's trend was penetrated (during the week) on the downside signaling the investor to move from an aggressive position (in the market) to a defensive position (out of the market and into T-Bills). A change in the risk index from a negative to a positive number during the week ending October 16 signals the investor to move from a defensive position to an aggressive position.

• **Using the Y-Process as a trading strategy?** In the 48-week example provided, if you were a buy-and-hold investor your gain would have been 13.53%.

If you were Y-Process user, you would have been "long the market" except for the 11 weeks between August 1 and October 15, 1998 when the risk indexes were negative. During that time you were out of the market and in Treasury Bills. Your funds grew at a T-bill rate of return of 3.85% for 11 weeks or 3.85% * 11/52 = .8%. In addition, with your being out of the market during these 11 weeks prevented you from taking a loss of 6.25%. This is what is called the "opportunity cost" had you remained in the market. Add .8% to your opportunity cost and your net opportunity cost is 7.05%. As a Y-Process investor, your net gain for the 48 weeks is an outstanding 7.05%+13.53% or 20.53%.

There is a caveat to this significant net gain. The analysis does not take into account transaction cost or tax costs. If your account is a tax-deferred type then tax cost will be deferred until you withdraw your funds.

As an exercise, try duplicating some of the risk numbers and Y-Process numbers found in the Table 9.1 using these equations 9.1 and 9.2.

Why does the Y-Process work so well? The answer lies in two fundamental factors: First, *all* trading decisions are the automatic result of *price action of the stock market* without any consideration to fundamental, economic or political factors. Although theorems and yield curves and advance/decline lines are valuable instruments, in the end, a market rises or falls on the unpredictable and unquantifiable emotions of humans. That's worth remembering, especially now, when many of the world's markets are newly liberated and many of the three billion investors are feeling, for the first time, the power of the popular will.

Table 9.1 Using The Y-Process Strategy To Optimize Returns
and Minimize Market Risk

1998 Friday's Close	S&P 500 Index	Y-Process number Y	Risk Index (R in %)	1999 Friday's Close	S&P 500 Index	Y-Process number Y	Risk Index (R in %)
7/3	1146	1100	4.1	1/1	1229	1147	6.7
7/10	1164	1107	4.9	1/8	1275	1162	8.8
7/17	1187	1117	5.9	1/15	1263	1174	7.0
7/24	1141	1120	1.9	1/22	1225	1180	3.7
7/31	1111	1120	0.1	1/29	1280	1192	6.9
8/7	1089	1116	-2.5	2/5	1239	1198	3.6
8/14	1063	1110	-4.4	2/12	1230	1202	2.3
8/21	1081	1107	-2.4	2/19	1239	1206	2.6
8/28	1027	1098	-6.9	2/26	1238	1210	2.3
9/4	974	1083	-11.2	3/5	1275	1218	4.5
9/11	1009	1075	-6.5	3/12	1295	1227	5.2
9/18	1020	1068	-4.7	3/19	1299	1236	4.9
9/25	1045	1066	-2.0	3/26	1283	1241	3.2
10/2	1003	1058	-5.5	4/2	1294	1248	3.6
10/9	984	1050	-6.7	4/9	1348	1260	6.6
10/16	1057	1051	0.6	4/16	1319	1267	4.0
10/23	1071	1053	1.7	4/23	1357	1277	5.9
10/30	1099	1059	3.7	4/30	1335	1284	3.8
11/6	1141	1068	6.4	5/7	1345	1292	4.0
11/13	1126	1075	4.5	5/14	1338	1297	3.0
11/20	1164	1086	6.7	5/21	1330	1301	2.2
11/27	1192	1098	7.8	5/28	1301	1301	0.0
12/4	1177	1108	5.9				
12/11	1166	1115	4.4				
12/18	1188	1124	5.4				
12/25	1226	1136	7.4				

Second, the ability to convert *human sentiment into numbers* which, in turn, can be manipulated by a computer. It's the computer's use of market price action that is caused by trades of individual investors in a free and open marketplace—for each buyer (demand) there must be a seller (supply). Hundreds of millions of shares are traded each day and at the close of the business-day, the *market's final price provides the consensus of the day's sentiment.* An analogy is that of a daily "Gallup-poll" of all stock buyers and sellers. A small change in the market's closing number would indicate that the consensus is slightly bullish or bearish, whereas a large change would indicate a very bullish or bearish mood.

The market is truly a caldron for all human emotions. The market ebbs and flows because of investor's dreams and hopes, disappointments and failures, and reactions to world events. This complete spectrum of investor emotions can be aggregated into swings between *anxiety and confidence,* with occasional side trips to *euphoria and fear.* Still, these market drivers do not preclude the development of a computer model that takes advantage of the very statement of sentiment (demand-supply differential) that the market makes each day. *The paradox is that the Y-Process' empirically derived mathematical formula eliminates the very basis that drives the market— human emotion.* The Y-Process' model that embodies this capability reduces investor's risk, increases stock market profits and provides superior returns.

There is an old market adage that raises an additional concern: "The only thing constant about the stock market is change." Market "timers" hope that the patterns in the system will work in the future. I confidently believe that—as history has amply demonstrated—*human emotion* will not change; it is the *one constant* in the stock market that we can count on.

---

1 In 1998, for the first time, there were two billion shares traded on the "big board" (NYSE). Theoretically, this represented four billion individual trades.

10

The Y-Process Managed S&P 500
Consistently Outperforms The Market

USING THE Y-PROCESS TO MANAGE YOUR STOCK PORTFOLIO ENABLES YOU TO CONSISTENTLY OUTPERFORM AN UNMANAGED (BUY-AND-HOLD) PORTFOLIO AND AT REDUCED RISK.

Validating The Y-Process. The question posed in this chapter is: "How can I prove that the Y-Process equations provide superior market results consistently while simultaneously reducing my risk?" The results in Tables 10.1 and 10.2 provide the detailed empirical evidence that the Y-Process consistently outperforms the stock market. I use the S&P 500 composite stock Index (the Index) as the stock market's benchmark for measuring these results.

The technique used to verify the Y-Process model is the same as used by engineers and scientists when they want to measure the affect that a new design or computer program model has on an existing process. The term engineers use for this comparative evaluation is called "backtesting." At its simplest, the backtesting technique is a side-by-side comparison of the stock market results by two investors. The first investor is a *buy-and-hold-forever* investor I call "Bahf," who buys $1000 of the Index. The second investor, I call "Ypro," also invests $1000 in the Index but uses the Y-Process model to time when to buy and when to sell the Index. The rules that Ypro uses for investing are simple. Either she is totally invested in the Index, or when designated by the Y-Process model, she moves her money into the money market, the equivalent of Treasury-bills. Both Bahf and Ypro invest their $1000 in the index on January 2, 1930 and every year thereafter they compare the value of their assets. This backtesting comparison continues for 70 years and terminates on December 31, 1999.

• **A sample of backtesting; comparison and results.** Table 10.1 contains the S&P 500 Index for 1930. It presents the Index's weekly closing price, the Y-Process' number and the Risk Index (RI) for each of the 52 weeks. Note that Bahf's annual return for the year was negative, i.e.,—27.74%, whereas Ypro had an exceptional year by comparison with a whopping 14.23% return.

If you scan down the risk index column, you can see that Ypro had two round-turns for the year. A round-turn is defined as a complete trading loop, that is, a combination of buying and selling the same number of shares of stock. In the table, the first sale occurs during the first week in May. Ypro sold her stock at 24.00 (the Y-Process number) providing a significant four month profit of 12.97%. The funds from the sale are moved into a money market (equivalent to T-bills) which yields 1.22% annually.

In accordance with the Y-Process' trading rules, when the Y-Process number is penetrated again, this time to the upside; the funds are moved out of the money market and are used to buy back the stock. Table 10.1 indicates that Ypro bought back her stock in three weeks at 23.97. However, Ypro received more stock for the same amount of money. Shortly thereafter Ypro sells her shares at 24.04 again due to a Y-Process downturn during the first week in June netting Ypro a gain of .32%. Ypro remains sidelined for the rest of the year. Ypro nets an annual return of

16.43% (excluding any fees, taxes and trading costs). Ypro is very pleased because she made a significant profit compared to Bahf who *lost* 21.37% for the year.

The interesting fact about the Y-Process is that when you sell your stock, the Y-Process does not predict how long you will be out of the market. What it does do is to project one week in advance, a Y-Process number that, when penetrated, signals a market turn with a high probability.

Table 10.1 S&P 500 Composite Stock Index and Y-Process Number for 1930

Date -(Friday)	S&P500 Index Price	Y-Process Number	Risk Index (RI)	Ypro buy(B) or sell(S)	Y-Process values	Annual Return (AR)*	Annual Total Return (ATR)**	
01/03/1930	21.23	21.18	0.00	B0	21.23			AR-ATR
01/10/1930	21.55	21.23	1.51%		1930 S&P 500= -27.74%	-21.37%		6.37%
01/17/1930	21.31	21.24	0.34%		Y-Process= 14.23%	16.44%		2.21%
01/24/1930	22.04	21.33	3.20%		1930 T-Bill= 1.22%			
01/31/1930	22.79	21.51	5.63%		Div= 6.37%			
02/07/1930	22.97	21.68	5.61%		Market Risk= 34.62%			
02/14/1930	23.35	21.88	6.29%		Rnd Turns = 2.0			
02/21/1930	22.92	22.01	3.99%					
02/28/1930	23.38	22.17	5.18%				Year	Index	Process
03/07/1930	23.59	22.34	5.31%				1930	-21.37%	16.43%
03/14/1930	23.45	22.47	4.17%				1931	-37.00%	5.82%
03/21/1930	24.29	22.69	6.60%				1932	-7.89%	38.20%
03/28/1930	24.85	22.94	7.67%				1933	50.97%	75.99%
04/04/1930	25.54	23.25	8.96%				1934	32.11%	14.90%
04/11/1930	25.84	23.56	8.83%				1935	44.90%	54.43%
04/18/1930	25.75	23.82	7.50%				1936	32.11%	34.54%
04/25/1930	25.32	24.00	5.22%	B0'	23.98 rate= 12.97%		1937	-30.97%	6.34%
05/02/1930	23.57	23.95	-1.61%	S1			1938	28.42%	33.70%
05/09/1930	23.69	23.92	-0.98%	S1'	RoR/t-bill= 0.07%		1939	-21.37%	16.43%
05/16/1930	24.28	23.97	1.29%	B1	23.94			
05/23/1930	24.03	23.98	0.22%					
05/30/1930	24.49	24.04	1.84%	B1'	24.02 rate= 0.32%			
06/06/1930	23.52	23.98	-1.96%	S2				
06/13/1930	22.26	23.78	-6.83%					
06/20/1930	20.25	23.37	-15.39%					

						Mkt Risk	R/Turns
06/27/1930	19.18	22.88	-19.27%				
07/04/1930	20.25	22.57	-11.46%		1930	34.62%	2.0
07/11/1930	20.55	22.33	-8.68%		1931	13.46%	2.5
07/18/1930	21.77	22.27	-2.30%		1932	23.08%	3.5
07/25/1930	21.50	22.18	-3.17%		1933	59.62%	4.0
08/01/1930	21.11	22.06	-4.49%		1934	40.38%	4.0
08/08/1930	20.27	21.85	-7.79%		1935	75.00%	1.0
08/15/1930	20.70	21.72	-4.91%		1936	88.46%	2.0
08/22/1930	20.79	21.61	-3.94%		1937	26.92%	2.5
08/29/1930	21.37	21.58	-1.00%		1938	42.31%	2.5
09/05/1930	21.34	21.56	-1.02%		1939	38.46%	6.0
09/12/1930	21.50	21.55	-0.24%				
09/19/1930	20.68	21.45	-3.73%				
09/26/1930	19.43	21.22	-9.19%	AVE ROUND TURNS FOR 30s =3			
10/03/1930	19.42	21.01	-8.17%	AVE Round Turns FOR 40s =3.15			
10/10/1930	18.11	20.67	-14.12%	AVE Round Turns FOR 50s =2.35			
10/17/1930	17.16	20.26	-18.05%	AVE Round Turns FOR 60s =2.9			
10/24/1930	17.74	19.96	-12.53%	AVE Round Turns FOR 70s =3.65			
10/31/1930	16.94	19.61	-15.76%	AVE Round Turns FOR 80s =3.4			
11/07/1930	16.09	19.20	-19.31%	AVE Round Turns FOR 90s =3.2			
11/14/1930	16.89	18.93	-12.06%	70 yrs ave. Round Turns =3.12			
11/21/1930	17.20	18.73	-8.87%				
11/28/1930	16.85	18.51	-9.83%				
12/05/1930	16.43	18.26	-11.16%				
12/12/1930	15.43	17.93	-16.22%	*AR excludes dividends but includes T-bill interest.			
12/19/1930	15.39	17.64	-14.59%	*ATR includes dividends and interest.			
12/26/1930	14.85	17.31	-16.56%				
12/31/1930	15.34	17.08	-11.34% S2'	RoR/t-bill= 0.73%			

- **Risk aversion using the Y-Process.** There are many ways of defining risk and there are elements of risk in every investment. In essence, anything that causes your investment to behave differently from what you'd expect can be called risk. Because risk is not one-dimensional, there is no single definition or measurement that can provide an accurate picture of an investment's total risk for every person. For the purpose of this book, I define risk for Y-Process users as the percentage of time you are in the market each year. Thus, any time you are in the market you are at 100 percent risk and when you are out of the stock market and in the money market (T-bills or equivalent) you are at zero risk.

At the top-center of Table 10.1, there is a group of numbers that contains a summary of 1930's statistics. One of these is "market risk" which has a value of 34.62%. Using my definition of risk, 34.62% represents 18 weeks of being in the market during the year, while ensconced in T-bills for the balance of the time. All interest accumulated from the 34 weeks while in the market is added to the dividends received from stock ownership during that period of time.

• **Other backtesting exhibits.** To portray the 70 years' results in table format would take up an excessive number of pages in this book. Instead, I have included in Appendix A through E the first year of each of the six remaining decades. These exhibits use the same format as Table 10.1. The upper right corner of each exhibit contains a summary of the annual total returns for the S&P Index and compares it with a Y-Process managed S&P Index. Also included are the market risk and round-turns for each year.

Summary Of 70 Years Of Backtesting Results.

Table 10.2 contains a summary of annual returns from 1930 through 1999. The table compares the performance of Bahf, the buy-and-hold-forever investor, who uses the S&P 500 Index with the performance of Ypro, the investor who uses a Y-Process managed Index. The table also provides two sets of annualized returns (five and ten year) for Bahf and Ypro. The table also contains the annual risk Ypro takes during the time she is in the market during that year. The risk number provides the percentage of 52 weeks that Ypro remained in the Index. The last column in the table provides the number of round-turn trades Ypro made during the year. The greater the number the more transaction cost that Ypro has to pay. In 1954 Ypro had no transaction cost because she stayed fully invested for the year and thus had the same annual return as Bahf. On the other hand, in 1994 Ypro made eight round-turns (a maximum for the 70 years). Even with all these trades, she still outperformed Bahf by five-fold. On average, there are only 3.2 round-turns per year.

Analyzing Table 10.2 Data. Boundary conditions, assumptions and caveats must be established before one can evaluate this data:

1. The first assumption is that the difference between the annual returns of Ypro and Bahf must be equal to or greater than one and one-half percent to be "statistically relevant." Anything less than this is considered a stalemate and is not used in the calculation for over- or underperformance relative to Bahf.

Table 10.2 70 Years of S&P 500 Backtesting For the Bahf and Ypro Investors.

Year	S&P 500 annual returns (%)	Y-Process-managed annual returns (%)	Unmanaged S&P 500 five-year return, annualized (%)	Y-Process-managed S&P 500 five-year return, annualized (%)	Unmanaged S&P 500 ten-year return, annualized (%)	Y-Process-managed S&P 500 ten-year return, annualized (%)	Annual reduction in risk using the Y-Process risk (%)	Number of "Round-Turns" per year using the Y-Process
1930	-21.37	16.43					63.46	1
1931	-37.00	5.82					86.54	3
1932	-7.89	38.20					76.92	4
1933	50.97	75.99					40.38	4
1934	-1.19	14.90	-7.41	28.05			59.62	4
1935	44.90	54.43					25.00	1
1936	32.11	34.54					21.54	2
1937	-30.97	6.34					73.18	3
1938	28.42	33.70					47.69	3
1939	-.01	17.99	11.15	28.37	1.45	28.21	61.54	6
1940	8.95	8.63					71.15	5
1941	9.67	7.60					69.23	3
1942	18.42	23.89					40.38	1
1943	24.70	29.37					36.54	4
1944	18.63	17.97	15.92	17.19			15.38	5
1945	34.53	32.23					9.62	3
1946	-7.26	9.84					57.69	3
1947	5.52	9.38					61.54	4
1948	5.49	15.45					51.92	5
1949	17.05	21.63	10.20	17.41	13.03	17.30	48.08	1
1950	28.98	28.87					13.46	2
1951	22.39	23.81					25.00	3
1952	17.07	17.93					26.92	4
1953	-.78	5.32					50.00	3
1954	49.30	48.49	22.31	24.09			1.00	0
1955	30.01	32.11					5.77	2
1956	6.35	13.72					48.08	5
1957	-9.83	10.36					59.62	2
1958	41.24	38.73					13.46	2
1959	11.54	13.78	14.45	21.22	18.32	22.65	23.08	1
1960	.38	9.49					55.77	5
1961	25.95	24.65					7.69	3
1962	-8.43	14.02					59.62	2
1963	21.93	21.50					7.69	1
1964	15.92	15.73	10.35	16.95			7.69	2
1965	12.00	14.36					21.15	2
1966	-9.52	6.17					67.31	4
1967	23.12	24.44					13.46	4
1968	10.62	17.23					26.92	4
1969	-7.93	9.38	4.91	14.14	7.60	15.54	76.92	4

30.19

70 years Of Backtesting Results (continued).

Year	S&P 500 Annual Returns (%)	"Y-Process" Managed Annual Returns (%)	Unmanaged S&P 500 five-year return, annualized (%)	Y-Process-managed S&P 500 five-year return, annualized (%)	Unmanaged S&P 500 ten-year return, annualized (%)	Y-Process-managed S&P 500 ten-year return, annualized (%)	Annual reduction in risk using the Y-Process risk (%)	Number of "Round-Turns" per year using the Y-Process
1970	3.51	23.25					61.54	1	15.05
1971	13.80	19.59					34.62	5
1972	18.30	20.15					19.23	7
1973	-13.91	7.84					69.23	3
1974	-24.47	13.35	-1.96	16.70			88.46	3
1975	35.63	41.63					25.00	3
1976	22.92	13.40					21.15	3
1977	-6.59	9.27					80.77	4
1978	6.34	19.94					51.92	2
1979	15.02	21.16	13.75	21.79	5.61	18.63	28.85	4
1980	30.31	36.53					23.08	2
1981	-4.32	16.64					63.46	6
1982	19.64	36.72					51.92	2
1983	21.57	26.30					25.00	4
1984	5.90	16.66	13.94	26.25			55.77	5
1985	30.07	33.47					19.23	3
1986	18.04	22.47					19.23	3
1987	5.60	33.29					28.85	3
1988	15.90	16.53					42.31	6
1989	30.38	29.98	19.63	26.97	16.75	26.61	7.69	2
1990	-2.90	12.44					65.38	5
1991	29.24	33.76					17.31	5
1992	7.30	8.81					21.15	4
1993	9.76	9.92					11.54	5
1994	1.33	8.31	8.41	14.27			48.08	8
1995	36.35	36.35					1.00	1
1996	22.27	22.69					11.54	2
1997	32.55	34.74					13.46	2
1998	27.85	37.52					21.15	2
1999	19.53	23.11	26.99	30.13	14.33	22.20	18.31	4

70 Yr Average (round turns) = 3.2

Note 1. An average of 39.3% of less risk is the equivalent of 20.5 weeks out of the market.

Note 2. An average of 3.3 Round-Turns per year costs the investor about $33/r-t or $110/yr.

2. The next assumption is that the stock price change on consecutive Fridays is a straight-line between the two closing values. The reason for this is to simplify the mathematical solution of determining when the Y-Process number is penetrated. This simplifying assumption allows the date and time of penetration to be determined by *interpolation*—a mathematical technique, used by many analysts and mathematicians, that estimates a value between two known values.

3. Because of the straight-line assumption between consecutive Fridays, intraday and intraweek whipsaws cannot occur using historical data. However, in actuality, whipsaws do happen in the market and they can have a significant impact when using the Y-Process as your investment strategy. There are certain rules that have been developed to mollify the impact of whipsaws when using the Y-Process. These will be discussed in detail in the next chapter.

4. For the purpose of comparing "apples with apples," the analysis does not take transaction costs, fees or taxes into account. Since these costs can turn out to be significant in reducing the returns, the topic of cost containment will also be covered in the next chapter.

Conclusions drawn from 70 years of backtesting. Table 10-3 summarizes the empirical results of backtesting 70 years of the Index. Using the first assumption of the boundary conditions established above, 15 years of return stalemates, i.e., ties are excluded. An analysis of the remaining 55 years of returns indicates that the Y-Process *outperforms* Bahf in 53 of the 57 years, yielding an accuracy of 93 percent in successfully calling market turns to increase investors' profits. These statistics are startling!

In examining Bahf's and Ypro's returns in detail, Bahf had 15 years of negative annual total returns of greater than 1.5 percent. This compares to *none* for Ypro. In the 70 years of backtesting, there were only four years—1941, 1945, 1958, and 1976—that Ypro underperformed Bahf and three of those were less than a 2.5 percent difference. The significance of these outstanding Y-Process results cannot be overstated.

The Table 10-3 provides two columns of additional attributes. The first is a measure of Y-Process' risk exposure. The smaller the number the lower the risk. The second is the average number of round-turns it takes to obtain the Y-Process' outstanding annual gains. The costs involved for an average of three round-turn trades is small relative to the gains obtained.

Table 10-3. Using The Y-Process Managed S&P 500 Versus Using A Passive Strategy.

Number of ties* of the Y-Process managed S&P 500 and the Buy-and-Hold S&P 500 Index	15
The number of times the Y-Process managed S&P 500 *outperformed* the S&P 500 Index.	51
The number of times the Y-Process managed S&P 500 *underperformed* the S&P 500 Index.	4
Total number of years.	70
The number of *negative* annual total returns of the S&P 500 Index in 70 years.	16
The number of *negative* annual total returns of Y-Process in 70 years.	*None*
The ave. annual reduction in risk exposure of the Y-Process managed S&P 500 in 70 years.	29%
The average market risk of the benchmark S&P 500 in 70 years.	100%
The average round-turns per year using the Y-Process in 70 years.	3.29

*A tie occurs if the difference between the Y-Process managed S&P 500 and the S&P 500 Index returns is less than ±1.5%.

Comparing The Y-Process With The Efficient-market Theory. Chapter Eight discussed the three schools that are followed today for investors to make a profit. The school of technical analysis used mechanical rules to look for recurring patterns in such things as trading volume, price movements, and odd-lot trading. From these patterns—the results of opinions and actions of those in the market—technicians hope to determine the beginnings of a change in prices and to profit from it.

The school of efficient markets had a major impact on technical analysis. Before the advent of the efficient-market theory, most market analysts were divided between the two schools—fundamental and technical analysis. Fundamental analysts look to basic economic factors to estimate the intrinsic value (the expected risk and return) of any given security. Technical analysts, on the other hand, believe that all the markets' opinion is summed up in the behavior of investors. This behavior is reflected in the prices and the enthusiasm with which the stocks are bought (volume). Technical analysts hope to improve their investment returns by trading on what they believe is investor's lack of historical perspective: They believe investors overbuy, oversell, and repeat their mistakes.

In the school of efficient markets, rule one states that investors cannot expect to beat the averages consistently. Technically, the backtesting results demonstrated that the Y-Process did not "consistently" outperform the market over the years—*if* one uses the definition of 100% of the time. However, one of Webster's definitions of *consistent* is "marked by steady regularity." Since Ypo "outperformed" Bahf 96 percent of the time over a 57-year time span, I consider this pretty consistent. Moreover, Ypro *never had a losing year* whereas Bahf had 16. I consider these statistics very compelling and dependable enough to provide a Y-Process investor with a strategic investment tool that by far exceeds a strategy of buying and holding the market.

While the efficient-market theory dampened enthusiasm for technical analysis for some time, I believe that this unique form of technical analysis—the Y-Process—will be discovered and used by investors for market timing of their individual portfolios. The distinguishing and yet paradoxical feature of the Y-Process is that it is based on the fundamental premise of the efficient-market theory; that is, each firm's security valuation is efficiently established because the marketplace is opened to all investors and information flows quickly without restrictions to all investors.

Can The Efficient-Market Theory Coexist With The Y-Process? The answer to this question is no. This may surprise you after the previous statement about the market's efficiency in setting a security's value. The empirical results of backtesting the Y-Process have provided sufficient evidence that an investor who uses the Y-Process can time the "market." Interestingly, when including ties, a Y-Process market timer has a 94 percent chance (66/70) to be equal to or outperform the market based on historical evidence.

• **How can the Y-Process beat the market?** All the mathematics thus far flies in the face of rule one of the efficient-market theory, which states that "You can't beat the market consistently." Now we may quibble over the exact definition of consistency but by the ground rules previously established, the Y-Process successfully outperformed the "market" 51 out of 55 years in the last 70 years—excluding ties. Moreover, a tally of the average annual total returns over the last 40 years, indicates that the Y-Process had a momentous advantage in returns over a passive (buy-and-hold) strategy—20.7 to 11.8 percent. How can this be?

A reexamination of the efficient-market theory indicates that the problem rests with 1) a poor choice of terminology, and 2) a quantum jump in conclusions. The derivation of the efficient-market theory started with a sample model of a stock's valuation, which suggested that its value depends on a firm's earnings, its dividend policy, and the investors' required rate of return. According to this dividend-growth model, future dividends should be discounted back to the present to determine a stock's value. An alternate to the dividend-growth model is the use of P/E ratios and forecasted earnings to determine if the stock should be purchased. Both the dividend-growth model and the use of P/E ratios place emphasis on future earnings and dividends. Risk is also incorporated into the valuation of stock through the application of the capital asset pricing model. This CAPM model suggests that the greater the risk the more investors' expect as a return on their investment.

Financial securities are bought and sold in competitive financial markets. This competition as well as the rapid dissemination of information among investors and the rapid changes in security prices results in efficient security markets. The efficient-market theory suggests that the individual investor cannot expect to consistently outperform the market on a risk-adjusted return.

• **The problem with the efficient-market theory.** These previous two paragraphs illustrate the problem with the efficient-market theory. First, a firm's stock value is based on future earnings and dividends. This seems logical. Next, in the second paragraph we jump to "efficient security markets" which is undefined but the reader probably assumes they pertain to all the individual firm's stock because they have been "bought and sold in competitive financial markets." This also seems logical. However, the step takes a major leap; a hypothesis called the "efficient-market theory" which states that "the investor cannot expect to consistently outperform the market." What is this "market" that the hypothesis refers to? Is it the sum of all the firms' stocks listed on the exchanges or is it the DJIA, the S &P 500 or some other index? Does efficient-market mean that if individual firms are efficient then the sum of all firms—*the market*—has to be efficient? Apparently it does.

If this is the case, how could backtesting of the Y-Process outperform "the market?" There are two reasons why. The first is that the efficient-market theory is a misnomer. It really should be labeled as the "efficient-securities theory" because the efficiencies apply to a firm's security not to the market as a whole. The second reason is that the Y-Process does not treat the "market" as if it were an individual firm's stock. If it were treated like a stock what would the "market's" valuation be? What dividend policy would the "market" have? What are the investors' required rates of return? If we could determine the S&P 500 Index's earnings or the

Wilshire 5000 Index's earnings would they be meaningful numbers? These are interesting questions especially when using the S&P 500 composite stock Index, as the market's proxy. It is an Index that is capitalization weighted. This means that the largest companies have the most impact on the index.

• **Why the Y-Process outperforms the market.** The Y-Process can call market turns successfully because it treats the S&P 500 differently than a stock. The Y-Process is successful in outperforming the market because the Index's model has characteristics and parameters that are different than an individual firm's stock. The S&P 500's earnings, dividend policy and growth potential are meaningless when it comes to determining whether the market's trend is about to change. What is important, is how the market's Index translates investor's emotions into numbers.

The heart of the Y-Process' market model is its use of price movement, which is caused by the trades of individual investors or money managers. For the market to work there must be a buyer for each seller and vice versa. Hundreds of millions of shares are traded each day and at the close of the business-day the market's final price provides the consensus of the day's sentiment. A small change in the market's closing number would indicate that the consensus is slightly bullish or bearish, whereas a large change would indicate a very bullish or bearish mood.

The market is truly the caldron for all human emotions; it is the ebb and flow of all dreams and fears, euphoria and anxiety, hopes and disappointments, reactions to world events and especially to federal reserve board announcements. But this does not preclude the development of an investment model, which takes advantage of the very *statement of sentiment* that the market makes each day. The Y-Process is a technical model, which has reduced investor's risk, increased stock market profits and provided superior returns. The paradox here is that the Y-Process model *eliminates* the very basis that drives the market, that is, *human emotion.*

In sum, this chapter has provided sufficient empirical evidence that the Y-Process outperforms the market on a consistent basis, and that this results in greater returns. Does this prove that the school of efficient markets is flawed? It must, because axiom one of the efficient-market theory says that "You can't beat the market consistently."

Is There Another Way Out Of This Dilemma For Those Who Want To Keep Both The Efficient—Market Theory And The Y-Process? Perhaps,

but the Y-Process must be considered as another anomaly? Unfortunately, the Y-Process cannot be explained away like the previously described six anomalies of the efficient-market theory. On the other hand, academia created a home for the six anomalies that has been recognized thus far and identified in Chapter Eight. The homes for these anomalies are called *the three versions of the efficient-market theory*: 1) the "strong form," 2) the "semi-strong form," and 3) the "weak form".

However, the Y-Process does not fit in any of these forms either. At this stage there is no mathematical proof other than empirical backtesting that the Y-Process challenges the efficacy of the efficient-market theory. I don't believe the world of financial academia is prepared to admit a paradigm shift in their fundamental dogma. However, the backtesting results presented above are hard to refute or deny. In order to retain the efficient-market theory *and* explain the consistent outperformance capability of the Y-Process, there may be one additional way; I propose a new version of the efficient-market theory—the fourth version—the *very weak form*.

The *very weak form** of the efficient-market theory asserts that a unique market-timing program called the Y-Process performs superior investment results. The Y-Process derives its data only from the stock portfolio's past

---

* (Unfortunately, this version of the efficient-market theory contradicts its axioms 1,3, and 4).

history. When this data is applied to the Y-Process model (Equations 9.1 and 9.2 in Chapter 9), the portfolio's Y-Process number and the following week's market Risk Index are determined. When the portfolio's value causes the risk index to change its sign from a negative to a positive value or from a positive to a negative value, this causes a Y-Process trading signal to be issued. An investor trading on this signal will, with a high likelihood, obtain superior market results.

Caveat: Before you rush out to take advantage of the *very weak form* of the efficient-market theory, you should remember several sobering considerations.

• First, the empirical results are only that, they do not *prove* the Y-Process' existence.

• Second, total transaction costs are important. These costs include, fees, commissions, sale charges, and taxes (if applicable) on dividends and capital gains. You must pay the transaction costs associated with this strategy and it's possible that transaction costs could exceed any excess return. (This will be discussed in the next chapter).

• Third, you must still select a stock market index, mutual fund or create your own portfolio. There is no assurance that the index/fund selected or portfolio created will outperform the market benchmark in that particular year although the probability is high if the index/fund selected is the S&P 500 benchmark or an S&P 500 mutual fund.

• Fourth, for this form to be useful for an active investment strategy, its signal must be transferable to you in a *timely fashion* to act on it.

• Fifth and last, for anyone to take advantage of the inefficiency it must be ongoing. Once the inefficiency is discovered and enough investors seek to take advantage of it, there is a possibility that the inefficiency *may* disappear. (This will be discussed in the next chapter).

In conclusion, I believe that in today's cost-conscience stock market environment, the Y-process overcomes all of these negatives. I also believe that the Y-Process will be officially accepted by academia, but not necessarily as the seventh anomaly to the efficient-market theory.

11

Getting Started

THE OLD ADAGE "THE DEVIL IS IN THE DETAILS" APPLIES WHEN TRYING TO OPTIMIZE YOUR GAINS. THIS CHAPTER CONTAINS RECOMMENDATIONS FOR HONING YOUR Y-PROCESS SKILLS ON: WHAT TO BUY, HOW TO TRADE, REDUCING COSTS, DEALING WITH WHIPSAWS AND OTHER SUBTLETIES THAT WILL BOOST YOUR AFTER-TAX RETURNS.

Investors Entering The New Millennium May Be Wealthier But Many Won't Nearly Be All That Wiser. Financial experts say we should combine a host of stocks and bonds and then focus on the performance of the entire portfolio. In theory, it's a smart strategy: By buying a slew of investments, some of which will soar while others are sinking, we should get healthy returns with less violent portfolio swings. The problem is, it doesn't correspond to people's intuition of how to build portfolios. The notion that you should consider portfolios as a whole and focus only on the risk and return of the *overall* portfolio is good advice. But it's advice that investors find hard to take.

What's our problem? We tend to divide our money into different mental accounts. We fret about each investment's performance, rather than focusing on our whole portfolio. And we aren't consistent about risk. With some money, we yearn for safety. With other money, we hunger for riches. Sure we could fight these instincts. But it makes more sense to incorporate these mental quirks into our portfolios. Here's how:

• **Safety in numbers.** If you find stock investing really nerve-racking, you might want to buy a mutual fund that offers one-stop shopping. These funds combine a host of stocks from a variety of market sectors, so they provide a globally diversified portfolio in a single mutual fund. This way you don't have to be emotionally attached to each stock in that fund and somebody else will diversify the fund for you. Buying this type of fund means fewer investments and all you see is the big picture.

• **Split personalities.** On the other hand, most investors don't build one portfolio, as the experts suggest. Instead, we build many portfolios; each designed to meet a different goal. We have some money for emergencies. Other money is money that gives us a chance to dream about being rich, and so we buy the hottest issues and lottery tickets. We behave like the main character in *The Four Faces of Eve*—a story on a multiple-personality disorder—where there are four people inside of us, each pulling in a different direction. The problem is how do we mediate among these personalities.

One way is to divide your money into four mental accounts. There is your emergency money, which is in a money-market fund. There is your retirement money and a college portfolio for the kids, and this money is mostly in well-diversified stock funds. And then there's your fun-money account. This mental accounting isn't ideal; but the resulting portfolio should meet both you psychological and investment needs, as long as you are careful. In particular, watch out for two pitfalls.

First, make sure your overall mix of stocks, bonds and cash investments makes sense for someone of your age and risk tolerance. For instance, if your pot of emergency money is too big and your retirement nest egg relatively small, you may unintentionally end up with too many conservative investments.

Second, don't let your hunger for "blowout" returns hurt the rest of your portfolio. Your best bet is to designate a small portion of your portfolio as "fun money." Build speculative investing as a legitimate activity and put in enough safeguards that if you take a high-stakes gamble that doesn't work out, you don't end up hurting other layers in your portfolio.

• **The core and satellite approach boosts returns and reduces risk.** In pursuit of both safety and riches, many investors combine ultra-conservative investments with those that are extraordinarily risky. In a modified form, you can also use this notion within your stock portfolio. The idea is to own a core portfolio of an index fund, so that you guarantee that part of your stock market money earns the market's return. Then, to give yourself a shot at beating the market, you add a smattering of a Y-Process managed stock exchange-traded funds (SEFs). This pursuit of safety and riches is known as the "core and satellite" approach. It is a good example of downside *protection* and upside *potential*, even though the core doesn't really have a floor in absolute dollar terms. If you use the Y-Process to manage both the core fund and the satellite SEFs, you have a greater potential to enhance all returns and further reduce risk.

Understanding And Profiting From Stock Exchange-traded Funds. SEFs
have been around since 1993. "Spiders," WEBS," "DIAMONDS," along with other fanciful named offerings, e.g., "Cubes," form a new class of securities. SEFs' owe their popularity to the success of index investing. In the five years from 1994 through 1999, the average U.S. closed-end equity fund has returned 30 percent, compared to 15 percent for its actively managed rival. When you consider that SEFs are essentially index funds that trade like stocks, its easy to understand why they've already attracted $25b in assets.

That may be the only thing about SEFs that's easy to understand. The typical SEF product is not a closed-end fund: What it is, is a hybrid. As with a closed-end fund, you buy shares in a stock exchange-traded fund from another shareholder on the open market, rather than from the fund company itself. And because you buy through a brokerage company, you'll pay a commission on the purchase, whether you choose a full-service firm, one of the bargain basement discount firms, or one of the on-line organizations.

What you're buying, however, is a fund designed to track one of several indexes; SPDRs (pronounced spiders for Standard and Poors Depository Receipts) that tracks the S&P 500 Index; Cubes, so named because they trade under the symbol QQQ that track the Nasdaq-100 index that tracks the top 100 companies in the Nasdaq Composite index; Diamonds are pegged to the Dow Jones Industrial Average, taking its name from three letters in DJIA; Select Sector SPDRs trade individual indexes, such as those devoted to financial services, energy, and technology. And then there are the WEBS (for World Equity Benchmarks Shares) which track the single country indexes maintained by Morgan Stanley Capital International, against which most international fund managers' measure their performance. Both Select Sector SPDRs and WEBS will be discussed in greater detail in the following chapter.

• **Cost comparison.** To a large extent, these SEFs function like their open-end and closed-end relatives—except they are often less costly. For example, while the closed-end Japan Equity fund, has an expense ratio of 1.19 percent, the Japan WEBS weigh-in at 26 basis points lower. On the other hand, SPDRs have an expense ratio of 18 basis points just like Vanguard's 500 Index fund. It is expected that SEF costs will go lower when a new comer, Barclays, goes public with their "Ishares" in the spring of 2000. When the British banking behemoth Barclays joins the current lineup of 17 WEBS products, they plan to include a fund pegged to the S&P 500, in a clear attempt to take business away from Vanguard and the other brokerages, and enter the market with an expense ratio as low as 0.08 percent. This is a good example of the value of the competition in an open and free marketplace.

• **Dividend drag.** Interestingly, in 1998, the Vanguard 500 Index fund returned an average annual 23.97 percentage points, nearly 20 basis points *more* than the SPDR, even though the two products have identical expense ratios, and presumably, identical holdings. Is it possible that all "index funds" are not created equal? Yes, you can add significant value by actively managing the fund and executing your trades efficiently by reducing "dividend drag" which is one of the facets of Spiders that is seldom discussed.

Technically registered as a "unit investment trust," (UIT) rather than a mutual fund, a SPDR distributes dividends to shareholders the third Friday of every quarter. But, the SPDR's 500 companies pay their dividends more frequently than that. Because of the UIT structure, however, the SPDR is required to hold dividends it receives as cash rather than reinvest them into the fund, as a mutual fund can. This is why the Index fund can outperform the index it tries to replicate every time. You can say; "Oh, the difference is just 20 basis points a year." But, over time, this compounded growth can be significant.

A recent example of dividend drag is a comparison of the SPDRs and the S&P 500 Index which it seeks to replicate. In 1999, the SPDR trust closed its fiscal year with a 27.54 percent return that underperformed the Index by 32 basis points, for the same period. 18 of those 32 basis points were the SPDRs expense ratio and the 14 basis point's balance was dividend drag.

• **Tax Efficiency of SEFs.** One of the confusing aspects of the SEFs is that while the products are all touted as more tax-efficient than mutual funds—they are also touted as appealing to short term traders. This is because SEFs are constantly being repriced during the day, whereas mutual funds calculate their net asset value only once each day—at the close of the trading day.

Further, SEFs are more tax efficient than mutual funds, if sometimes narrowly. For the five years through 1998, owners of SPDR shares kept 95.84 percent of their return after paying off Uncle Sam compared with 95.45 percent for Vanguard 500 shareholders. It's true that pretax returns on Spiders were lower, due to dividend drag, but Barclays' S&P products will take care of that problem. Unlike Spiders, IShares are legally structured as a *mutual fund*, allowing them to reinvest dividends rather than hold dividends as cash.

Furthermore, most of the SEF products available now are structured as mutual funds, making dividend drag, well—not that much of a drag. This came about as the SEC granted "exemptive relief" after many SEFs petitioned the Commission to bypass certain restrictions that generally apply to mutual funds. Owners of SEF shares are now allowed to sell their shares short—an option not available to mutual fund shareholders. The next chapter will discuss this attribute and use it as the cornerstone of a tax-saving strategy.

• **"Payment in-kind" enhances tax efficiency.** This is a sophisticated strategy to eliminate unrealized capital gains. Mutual funds are expected to be ready, at any time, to give shareholders cash in exchange for their shares. SEFs, however, regularly redeem shares for a basket of stocks being turned-in and can issue shares in exchange for a similar basket.

From a practical standpoint, this feature doesn't matter to individual investors. After all, you're not buying or redeeming your shares from the fund company, and, in fact, the in-kind payments apply only to blocks of at least 50,000 shares. For SPDRs, that would represent about $7.5m at today's prices. However, it is precisely that in-kind feature that makes SEFs so tax efficient. If a large shareholder in your mutual fund decides to redeem their shares, your fund manager will almost certainly have to sell securities to raise the necessary cash, soaking you and your fellow remaining shareholders with not only the transaction cost but also—and more painfully—the taxable capital gains he may have to distribute.

By contrast, if a large owner of SPDRs—Fidelity for example—decides to sell some of its shares, it bundles up 50,000 of them into a "redemption unit" and hands this over to the fund, receiving a bunch of stock in return. Because the fund didn't sell this stock, but only swapped it, no taxes or capital gains are involved.

Table 11.1 Comparison of SEFs and Index mutual funds.

Stock Exchange -traded Fund	Index Mutual Fund
Tax-efficiency: Extremely high, due to the low turnover associated with index structure and the lack of redemption-induced sales.	83% (Ave.)
Expense Ratio: Domestic[1] .19%-.65%	.15%-1.5%
Expense Ratio: International[2] .95%-1.43%	.97% (Ave.)
Available for short-selling Yes	No
Pricing: Continuous	Once a day
Portfolio disclosure: Continuous	Twice a year
Where to buy: From any brokerage	From a brokerage, a fund supermarket, or directly from the fund company, depending on the fund.
Sales charge to trade: Yes	Varies
Minimum investment: Most SEFs sell for under $100	Average of $2,000

1. Most domestic SEFs trade at 18 basis points, a few at 25; Select Sector
   SPDRs, which track industrial indexes, have an expense ratio of
   approximately 65 basis points.
2. The Malaysia WEBS product has an unusually high (1.43%) expense ratio due
   to that country's capital controls.

Source: Morningstar

And it gets better. Every day, SEFs publish a list of the stocks, and
proportions of those stocks, that it will hand over in exchange for a
redemption unit. While it is limited to stocks in its index, within that
limitation it can arrange the basket however it likes. And it still gets better.
The SEF can identify not only the stocks it wishes to sell, but also the
specific shares.

• **Comparison of SEFs and index funds.** Table 11.1 contains an interesting comparison of the advantages and limitations of investing in SEFs

and Index mutual funds. One of the areas that the table does not comment on is the customer service an investor gets when calling a mutual fund representative using the fund's handy 1-800 telephone number.

Taking Control Of Brokerage Commissions. The effect of broker's costs will reduce your profits. For day traders, this can be a dominant factor. There are no round-turn costs when trading certain no-load funds, but this is not the case when trading SEFs or individual firms. By using a discount broker, you can get "advertised" stock trades that cost as low as $10 per round-turn.

Even in large brokerage firms, such as Fidelity Investment Company, the cost of trading stocks and SEFs is very competitive. At this writing, the total "round-turn" cost for Fidelity is a fixed fee or $33, i.e., $15 when buying and $18 when selling* up to 1000 shares. The prerequisite is that you must be a "preferred" client (12 trades per year) and you trade "Online"—via the Internet. This round-turn cost is relatively small when considering the round-turn cost of trading 1000 shares of a high value stock. For instance, the $33 round-turn cost of trading 1000 shares of $100 per share stock is 3 1/3 basis points (.033 percent). This is a rather low cost for the value of the transaction. There is an additional cost of $5 per trade if you place your trade at other than a "market order."

In comparison, trading the same number of shares using a "representative-assisted transaction," will cost a preferred client is $142, i.e., $71 when buying and $74 when selling. For limit and stop orders add $5 per trade.

Optimizing Your Trade Order Type. In order to buy and sell a security you must place an order through a stockbroker. This can be done by mail, phone, electronically (via the Internet) or in person. To complete an order,

---

* There is an additional SEC fee of $3 on all sales.

four essential questions that must be answered: 1) the price that you want to sell or buy the security, 2) the number of shares that you want to buy or sell, 3) the type of order, and 4) the "time in force." Each of these will be discussed in turn. There are three types of buy and sell orders: market orders, limit orders, and stop orders.

• **Type 1: Market orders.** When you place a *market order* you are instructing your broker to buy or sell securities for your account at the *next available price*. A market order remains in effect for the day only. When your stockbroker receives your market order, he forwards it to the specialist (market maker) at the appropriate stock market, e.g., AMEX, NYSE, and Nasdaq. There may be market orders ahead of yours, so the specialist (market maker) enters your order in queue in his "book." As the specialist fills the orders, you move up in queue until your market order is executed by *matching* your shares to buy (or sell) to another investor's order for shares to sell (or buy).

The advantage of a market order is that you are guaranteed a prompt execution of all your shares, as long as the security is actively traded and market conditions permit but *not at a specific price*. There is a disadvantage to sell shares using a market order in a down market because your order may be filled at a price considerably below the market value on the stock screen at the time you placed it. Some academics call this price difference "slippage."

• **Type 2: Limit orders.** *Limit orders* are inherently "*or better*" orders. The advantage of placing a limit order *to buy* makes the stock eligible to be purchased *at or below* your limit price, but *never above it*. The same advantage holds for placing a limit order to sell except that it makes the stock eligible to be sold *at or above* your limit price, but *never below it*.

There are also disadvantages to limit orders. Orders at each price level are filled in a sequence that is determined by the rules of the various exchanges. But, there can be no assurance that all orders at a particular price limit (including yours) will be filled when that price is reached. The reason? Such orders are subject to the existence of a market for that security. Thus, the fact that your price limit (or better) was reached does not guarantee an execution. In other words, you run the risk that the price will run away from your limit, because no buyers (or sellers) and therefore, your trade won't be executed.

• **Type 3: Stop orders.** *Stop orders* are used to buy or sell a stock *after* the stock has reached the "stop" price that you enter in your order. They are used in conjunction with loss and limit orders. Thus, there are two types of stop orders, a *stop loss order* and a *stop limit order*.

A buy-or sell-*stop loss order* automatically becomes a *market* order when the "stop" price is reached.

A buy-or sell-*stop limit order* automatically becomes a limit order when the "stop" price is reached.

Note: A buy stop order is generally used when you're "short the market"* and you want to "cover your short" position.

Stop Limit Orders Recommended For Y-Process Investors. When you buy or sell stocks, I recommend the use of stop limit orders because a limit order defends against poor execution of trades. If you are buying, place your stop limit at or just above the current asked price; the shares will be bought at this level or lower. If you are selling put your limit at the current bid price or just below; the stock will be sold at this stop price or higher. There is always the risk that the price will run away from your limit, and your trade won't be executed. If you're unwilling to take this risk then use a stop loss order.

• **Stop loss orders.** For a Y-Process investor to *buy* a stock using a *stop loss order,* you place a stop loss order at or above the current market in accordance with the Y-Process number. When the "stop" price is reached

---

* See glossary for definitions.

the stop loss order automatically becomes a market order to buy. Similarly, to *sell* a stock, you place a *stop loss order* at or below the current market. When the "stop" is reached, the stop loss order automatically becomes a market order to sell. In both of these cases, there is "slippage" potential when selling (or buying) shares using a market order. That is, your sell (or buy) order may be filled at a price well below (or above) the market value at the time the stop was reached.

• **Stop limit orders.** When you place a limit order to buy, that stock is eligible to be purchased at or below your limit price, but never above it. When you place a limit order to sell, that stock is eligible to be sold at or above your limit price, but never below.

A stop limit order automatically becomes a limit order when the stop price is reached. Like any limit order, a stop limit order may be filled in whole, in part, or not at all, depending on the number of shares available for sale or purchase at the time. In these cases, there is no "slippage" possible. But there is a possibility that the price will run away from your stop price. If this were to happen, it would most likely happen in thinly traded stocks.

• **Time in force.** Time in force is a term that describes the duration of a buy or sell order. There are six types of "time in force" entries: 1) Day, 2) Good 'til cancel), 3) Fill or Kill, 4) Immediate or cancel, 5) On the Open, and 6) On the close. When you place orders, you may place an order good only for the "Day" on which they are entered or for an open-ended period that ends when it is executed or when you cancel (GTC) or they expire, i.e., normally 120 calendar days after they are placed. An order may be placed before the market opens and with a criterion that it must be executed at the opening price. At any time prior to the close you may enter an order with a criteria that it must be executed at the closing price.

Limit orders for more than 100 shares or for multiple round lots (200, 300, 400, etc.) may be filled completely or in part until completed. It may take more than one trading day to completely fill a multiple round lot order unless the order is designated as one of the following types:

a). *Fill or Kill* (fill the order immediately or cancel it).

b). *Immediate or cancel* (fill the whole order or any part immediately, and cancel any unfilled balance).

• **Good 'til cancel.** An investor who places a *good 'til cancel order* when placing *Buy-* or *Sell-stop orders* can go on vacation without anxiety. This approach will mechanically control the process of either entering the market or selling the market as calculated using the Y-Process equations for the Y-Process value. However, these *stop orders* are valid for one week because the Y-Process requires weekly updates. Even if the investor is on vacation, the prudent thing to do in order to preserve your capital, is to follow the rules—update each stock in your portfolio and reenter the new *stop orders*.

Effects Of Short-term Whipsaws On Y-Process Investors.
If the Y-Process has an Achilles' heel it is whipsaws. Whipsaws generally happen in a sideward moving market and occur around the Y-Process transition of buying or selling; the term whipsaw is slang for the financial effect of a rapid upward price movement followed by a rapid decline. A whipsaw contains three attributes: 1) there must be round-turn trade involved, 2) the round-turn must occur is a short period of time, and 3) the round-turn trade must result in a loss.

When using the Y-Process trading strategy, being whipsawed is a sell signal quickly followed by a buy signal or vice versa. This test defines a whipsaw, if a round-turn trade occurred within one month of the original buy order. If the whipsaw occurred within the same week (intra-week), this I define as *a short-term whipsaw* (previously called a false alarm).

• **The psychological effect of whipsaws.** Being whipsawed can be devastating to some investors in three ways. First, it can be monetarily detrimental because whipsaws cause an investor to be exposed to financial risk on both the up- and downside of a round-turn transaction. It is possible that you are subjected to a double market loss through trying inopportunely to recoup a loss by a subsequent buy-back of the same security at a higher price than you sold it, and in a round-turn trade there is always the additional cost of the round-turn commissions.

Second, being whipsawed may have a severe negative psychological effect greater than the financial loss because it can cause you to lose faith in the Y-Process. One of the primary advantages of the Y-Process is that it provides the investor with a "non-emotional means of buying and selling stocks." Once you build a confidence factor that you will always protect your downside risk exposure with the Y-Process it becomes almost mechanical to buy and sell stocks and SEFs.

Third, the whipsaw can have other deleterious financial affects from a federal income tax viewpoint. The financial impact in *taxable brokerage accounts* can be much greater than the round-turn cost because trading stock held for less than 12 months is a short term transaction and that would cause a short term capital gain.

• **The Preservation Of Capital Rule.** As previously discussed backtesting the S&P 500 index was used to verify and validate the utility of the Y-Process in beating the market. The backtesting technique only allowed a single trade per week, because the database used only week ending stock prices. In other words, *intraweek* whipsaws could not occur in the 3500 weeks tested because the test examined the change in price from Friday to Friday. However, using the Y-Process in buying and selling index funds and SEFs in the stock market "real-time", short-term intraweek whipsaws can occur and do occur because stock market prices vary continuously on a daily basis. Moreover, in "real-time" stock markets, short term whipsaws are not limited to intraweek, they can and have occurred within the same day. These are called intraday whipsaws.

To replicate the stunning success of the 70 years of the "backtested" Y-Process, I developed a *preservation of capital rule* to prohibit short term (intraday or intraweek) whipsaws from occurring in the "real-time" market utilization of the Y-Process. The preservation of capital rule allows a single *sell* trade per week for a given stock portfolio, SEF or index fund. For example, if you buy an SEF on Monday and its price violates the Y-Process number any time during the week, you must sell it as soon as that event occurs. In accordance with the *preservation of capital rule*, the earliest you can repurchase this SEF is the following Monday. The preservation of capital rule prohibits you from buying back until the following Monday, preferrably mid-morning so that you can get a feel for what the market is doing. Of course if the market is in a steep decline, you have the option of waiting until the next day to buy.

12

Stretch Your Gains:
Reach For Higher Retruns

DOES A STRATEGY THAT AIMS FOR HIGHER RETURNS MEAN HIGHER RISK?
NOT IF YOU USE Y-PROCESS.

Aiming For Higher Returns. Financial academics argue that any strategy that aims for higher returns mean higher risks. They also caution investors to limit aggressive investments to a small portion of a well-diversified portfolio and *never* use money they can't afford to lose.

For the experienced, sophisticated Y-Process investor, this chapter presents a view that there is nothing wrong with reserving a portion of your portfolio to aim for higher returns. Even a few percentage points difference in return can have a big impact on how fast your money grows. For example, at the market's historical average return of about 11 percent a year, it takes a little over six and one-half years for your stake to double. Not bad; but if you can earn five percentage points more, or 16 percent yearly, your investment will double in four and one-half years (all before taxes of course).

In the paragraphs that follow, I describe four strategies that use the Y-Process in an aggressive and unique manner that could earn advanced investors 16 percent returns or more annually over the next five years or more years. Not all of these strategies will be right for you, but the better you understand them, the more likely you'll be able to select the right choice for you.

Strategy One. International Stock Exchange-Traded Funds From Amsterdam To Zurich.

"Indexing" is known for its market tracking performance. Index mutual funds are linked to the S&P 500 stock-index, Dow Jones Industrial Average, Nasdaq-100 or some other benchmark. When you bought an index fund, you knew your return would match that of the index it was tracking (less commissions and taxes).

As described in the previous chapter, *international* stock exchange-traded funds (SEFs), are a first cousin of index funds traded on the American Stock Exchange. This provides you the ability to purchase a benchmark of a country as easy as of a domestic company stock or fund. Since 1990, combined U.S. and international indexed mutual fund assets have increased greater than 31-fold. Investing only in the U.S. markets passes up about 60 percent of the world's equity market.

One reason for the popularity of international SEFs are that they work like an index fund, yet trades like a stock. You can track their performance real time just like a stock, and easily buy or sell during the trading day, through your broker or online. But unlike stock, you are not buying a single company, you're buying an entire stock index and getting the diversification of owning a stock in many companies. Unlike most managed funds, international SEFs offer an approach to investing that provides lower fees and expenses and important tax efficiencies. A single share lets you buy or sell the largest and most actively traded companies on each of the 17 country's' stock exchanges, all in one security.

WEBS Index Fund, Inc. is an American Stock Exchange-traded fund consisting of 17 foreign markets and their major local market indexes, such as Germany's DAX, and Japan's Nikkei 225. Table 12.1 contains a complete list of 30 Nasdaq/AMEX Indexes. The table includes the seventeen countries, their local market indexes and the symbol used to trade these WEBS. These WEBS provide individual investment results that correspond to the price and yield performance of their publicly traded securities, in the aggregate, as compiled by Morgan Stanley Capital International Index.

• **Advantages and limitations of SEFs.** Because you must pay a commission each time you trade, stock exchange-traded funds are not appropriate for investors using a dollar-cost-averaging strategy, or any similar discipline involving regular purchases of shares. The comparatively low share price of SEFs offers an opportunity for cash-strapped investors to gain exposure to other areas, such as, the international arena and specialized portfolios of specific industry sectors that might otherwise be out of the reach because of minimum investments demanded by many mutual funds. But, it's possible that the commissions on SEFs will eat into your return sufficiently unless you're prepared to invest a large enough sum to amortize them. On the other hand, this makes a very good case for you to trade using a computer. Trading via Internet provides most investors a significant discount in trading cost. This discount is enhanced considerably if your brokerage firm registers you as an active trader. Over time, the money saved should be sufficient to pay for the cost of the computer and the Internet interface.

• **Foreign investments involve greater risks than U.S. investments.** As with any investments, share price and return will fluctuate. The risks of foreign investments also include unstable political climates and economic uncertainties as well as the risk of currency fluctuations. When foreign securities are sold and converted back into U.S. dollars, the value of the dollars may have risen or declined, depending on what has happened in the foreign exchange markets. When trading WEBS however, the daily conversions are already built-in and the value of the daily share price are listed in U.S. dollars.

• **There are three classic advantages offered by foreign securities.** The first is investing in economies experiencing economic growth generally found in countries called "emerging markets." The second advantage is more obvious; it's risk reduction through diversification using global markets. Finally, there is the advantage of obtaining excess returns due to certain "inefficiencies" of foreign markets.

It is this last advantage that is both intriguing and risky. According to the school of efficient markets, higher returns can be achieved by bearing more risk, i.e., purchasing assets whose returns tend to be more *volatile* than the U.S. markets as a whole. Market inefficiencies suggest that astute investors and those who also manage their portfolio using the Y-Process may be able to isolate a foreign market that is "under- or overvalued." If this were true, then the opportunity for excess returns would exist.

WEBS are ideal for the disciplined Y-Process investor who has the stamina to dart-in and -out of the market using the Y-Process equations provided in Chapter 9. If these SEFs sound intriguing, soul-searching is recommended. It'll take plenty of discipline. Because some of these countries are "thinly traded," stop loss or limit orders are essential to prevent you from going into free-fall while you're not looking. Of course, this could be beneficial if you're on the "short-side" which you can do with SEFs.

Strategy Two. Investing In Niche (Sector) Funds. Have you ever wished that you owned some of those cyber stocks or technology stocks when they were the rage? Most sane investors conclude that the risks are too monumental to invest anything more than a small amount of "mad" money in such a narrow niche. Yet, while funds that focus on a particular industry are often quite volatile, the payoffs can be worthwhile.

If an investor started with $10,000 and earned just average returns in the top-performing sector for each of the 10 years beginning in 1989, there money would have grown to an outstanding $1.1 million, a compound return of 60 percent a year. Of course the risks are high too. If that same investor had purchased the worst performing sector for those 10 years, they'd have just $768 left, a compounded return of minus 23 percent each year.

Table 12.1 contains the eight. Clearly these funds are not for everyone. That's why sector funds tend to attract market timers. For the investor who has the discipline to manage his stock portfolios using the Y-Process, sector funds provide the potential of large returns while downside risk would be significantly reduced. If the investor follows the Y-Process' risk index alert, the timing of the sell signal will reduce risk and maximize returns.

• **Evaluating sector funds.** There are several ways to evaluate a fund's historical performance. The investor can look at the cumulative total percentage change in value, the average annual percentage change, or the growth of a hypothetical $10,000 investment. *Total Returns* reflects the change in value of an investment, assuming reinvestments of the fund's dividend income and capital gains (the profits earned upon the sale of securities) that account for those sales charges, commissions and trading fees.

Cumulative Total Returns shows the fund's performance in percentage terms over a set period, e.g., one year, five years and ten years. The investor can compare the funds to a baseline to evaluate relative performance. Many investors use the S&P 500-composite Index as the baseline.

Average Annual Total Returns take the funds' cumulative return and shows the investor what would have happened if the fund had performed at a constant rate each year.

• **Buying sector funds.** If you're interested in sector investing, there are two approaches. The first approach buys a special class of SEFs—select sector SPDRs. Table 12.1 contains the nine select SPDR sectors presently traded on the American Stock Exchange.

Table 12.1 Complete List of 30 Nasdaq/Amex Indexes and Symbols

MAJOR U.S. INDEXES

SPDRs "S&P Depository Receipts" (SPY)

S&P MIDCAP-400 (MDY)

NASDAQ-100 Shares "Cubes" (QQQ)

DOW-30 "Diamonds" (DIA)

INTERNET INDEXES

INTERNET INDEX (EMERGING MKTS TELECOMM) (ETF)

MERRILL LYNCH INTERNET INDEX (HHH)

SECTOR SPIDERS

—BASIC INDUSTRIES (XLB)

—CONSUMER SERVICES (XLV)

—CONSUMER STAPLES (XLP)

—CYCLICALS/TRANSPORTATION (XLY)

—ENERGY (XLE)

—FINANCIALS (XLF)

—INDUSTRIAL (XLI)

—TECHNOLOGY (XLK)

—UTILITIES (XLU)

WEBS (World Equity Benchmark Shares)	Local Market Index
—AUSTRALIA (EWA)	All Ordinaries
—AUSTRIA (EWO)	ATX

—BELGIUM (EWK)	BELFOX
—CANADA (EWC)	TORONTO 35
—FRANCE (EWQ)	CAC
—GERMANY (EWG)	DAX
—Hong Kong (EWH)	Hang Sang
—ITALY (EWI)	BCI
—JAPAN (EWJ)	Nikkei 225
—MALAYSIA (EWM)	KLSE
—MEXICO (EWW)	IPC
—NETHERLANDS (EWN)	EOE
—SINGAPORE (EWS)	Striaghts Times
—SPAIN (EWP)	IBEX
—SWEDEN (EWD)	OMX
—SWITZERLAND (EWL)	SMI
—UNITED KINGDOM (EWU)	FTSE

The second approach uses brokerage companies that deal in sector funds. The largest selections are offered by Fidelity, with 40 sector funds, Rydex, with 14, and Invesco and Morgan Stanley, with 11 apiece. Rydex and Invesco are load-free, whereas Fidelity and Morgan Stanley impose sales charges. Moreover, Fidelity also imposes a penalty of 3/4 percent on trading the sector within 90 days of the initial purchase. Table 12.2 provides the cumulative returns of Fidelity's 47 select portfolios for the year ended in February 1999.

Fidelity has a unique and cost savings exchange privilege when trading their sector funds. A special *Select Money Market* portfolio has been created as a "parking place" for each exchange out of one of the "select equity portfolios." This is ideally suited for the Y-Process investor, since fees do not apply to exchanges out of the Money Market. Three- percent fees once paid do not have to be paid again as this "loaded money" stays within sector fund family.

Table 12.2 Fidelity Sector Funds, Cumulative Returns
For The Year Ended 28 February, 1999.

Sector Fund Name	Cumulative Total Return (%)
Computers	66.4
Developing Communications	63.
Technology	55.7
Leisure	37.5
Multimedia	36.7
Retailing	36.7
Electronics	35.3
Software & Computer Services	32.6
Utilities Growth	32.2
Health Care	27.2
Biotechnology	27.1
Business Services & Outsourcing	26.2
Telecommunications	22.2
Medical Equipment & Systems	21.
Consumer Industries	20.2
S&P 500	19.74
Insurance	9.8
Financial Services	8.4
Food & Agriculture	7.8
Brokerage & Investment Management	4.7
Air Transportation	4.1
Regional Banks	3.1
Industrial Equipment	1.
Transportation	-1.7
Construction and Housing	-2.2
Cyclical Industries	-5.
Automotive	-8.5
Defense & Aerospace	-9.9
Precious Metals	-10.9
Gold	-15.7
Paper & Forest	-17.
Industrial Materials	-18.7
Home Finance	-19.1
Natural Gas	-19.2
Energy	-22.
Environmental Services	-22.2
Chemicals	-22.7
Natural Resources	-24.6
Medical Delivery	-29.5
Energy Services	-50.6

Strategy Three. Buying On Margin. Another way to use the capabilities of the Y-Process in pursuit of higher returns and reduced risk is to buy funds on margin, i.e., partly with money borrowed from your broker. Margin boosts both your risk and your potential reward. Buying on margin is a strategy that is not in the domain of investors who have "tax-deferred" stock portfolios. Tax deferred accounts like IRAs or other types of retirement plans generally are prohibited from buying on margin by SEC rules. For taxable accounts that's a different matter.

Here's how it works: Suppose that you are thinking of buying 100 shares of a SEF priced at $10 a share for $1,000. Instead of paying cash, you set up a margin account at your brokerage firm and purchase $2,000 of SEF shares, borrowing the extra $1,000. If the share price grows 50 percent, to $15, the investment rises to $3,000. After paying back the $1,000 you owe the broker, you'd have $2,000 left for a 100 percent profit (less interest on the loan). That's twice what you'd have made paying cash. Thanks to that boost, and even with the typical 7.5—9 percent interest that brokers charge for margin loans, your SEF shares would need to earn only about 11.5 percent a year for you to double your stake in five years, as opposed to the 15 percent you'd need without leverage.

Buying on margin can be a curse, though, if your stock plummets. Then that leverage will magnify your losses instead of your gains. Brokerages generally let you borrow up to half the cost of a fund, the most allowed by Federal Reserve Board rules. Past that, rules vary. Fidelity customers get a margin call—meaning they either have to put up more cash or sell some of their position—if the equity in an account dips below 30 percent of the market value of the securities. Schwab won't make that call until total equity dips below 30 percent.

For Y-Process investors, buying on margin has less of a threat of "losing your shirt" by being caught in a downside plunge. The reasons being that you get advanced notice of a potential decline or correction when the Y-Process number is violated.

Strategy Four. The "Market-Neutral Position." Sophisticated investors are always on the lookout for strategies to increase *net* gains. The market-neutral position does it by selectively "hedging your exposure" to reduce taxes. Ordinary income and short-term capital gains are taxed at your top federal rate. And, today's tax law requires that you pay short term capital gains at your standard tax rate schedule, i.e., 15 percent, 28 percent, 31 percent, 38 percent, or 39.6 percent. The 1997 tax law allows investors to pay a long-term capital gain tax at a *fixed* 20 percent rate for securities held a minimum of 18 months*.

Depending on your tax-bracket, this can significantly increase your after-tax returns. Thus, if you are in the 28 percent tax-bracket, you will save an additional 8 percent in taxes; a much more significant 19.6 percent saving could occur for securities held a minimum of 18 months, if you are in the 39.6 percent tax-bracket. As Ben Franklin said, "A penny saved is a penny earned." In this example, if you owned fund "X," its return has been increased by 19.6 percent by holding it for a year and one-half.

• **How does a market-neutral position work?** As a Y-Process investor you get a signal to sell your securities. Instead of selling fund X that you've owned for almost 12 months in a taxable account—providing a short- term capital gain profit—you try to hold on for an additional six months. To do this, you establish a market neutral position. How? By shorting the equivalent dollar amount of an *alias-fund*, which we'll call fund "Z." Fund Z has a high correlation to fund X. R^2 is a mathematical measurement, called a correlation coefficient, which provides information on how closely your fund's performance matches the performance of a benchmark index, such as fund Z. R^2 is a proportion which ranges between 0.00 and 1.00. An R^2 of 1.00 indicates perfect correlation to the benchmark index, i.e., if X goes

---

* Tax Relief Act of 1997; also contains a provision for 18 percent long term capital gain for assets purchased after 2000 and held for 5 years.

up 10 percent so does Z. If X goes down 3.5 percent so does Z. At the other end of the spectrum, a 0.00 R^2 indicates a zero correlation. Hence, the lower the R^2, the less the fund's performance tracks the benchmark index, Z.

• **An example of extending your gains using R^2.** Let's assume you own the SEF known as Spiders, symbol SPY. You have a significant short-term capital gain. If you could hold your Spiders for another six months, you will be able to make the critical time of holding the Spiders for 18 months, thus making your gains taxable at the "fixed" long-term capital gains rate of 20 percent. Unfortunately, your Y-Process indicator has just signaled that a downturn is eminent. You normally would sell out your position, but you have been told that Diamonds, symbol DIA, has a high R^2 to Spiders, a correlation of about .86. You decide to short an equal dollar amount of Diamonds against you Spiders. This market-neutral position allows you to ride out the potential six month melt-down preserving most of your gains because as your Spiders drop in value, your (shorted) Diamonds increase in value at an 86 percent rate. Not a perfect match, but if you hold on for six months, you can convert your Spider's gain to a fixed 20%-long term capital gain tax rate, with a net saving of 19.6 percent in taxes.

To complete the transaction, when your Spiders reach the critical maturity date, you sell them and you simultaneously cover your Diamonds short position closing out this transaction. Gains made on Spiders are paid at the long-term rate and any gains/losses on Diamonds are short-term capital gains/losses. If you have insufficient funds to perform this transaction, try borrowing money from your broker by margining the spider's shares.

• **Shorting against the box.** Why go through all this trouble? Why not just short the Spiders? The reason is that the IRS disallows this procedure, if the intent is to establish a long-term capital gain (which is exactly what our market-neutral position strategy is all about). The IRS has a term for this—"shorting-against-the-box"—i.e., taking a short position on a stock you already own. However, if an investor shorts a similar type of equity, such as an *alias-stock or fund* that is not *substantially the same as the equity the investor's holding,* then the IRS does not consider this to be a short-against-the-box

The key to this market-neutral position strategy is (1) finding the appropriate high correlation stock or fund or SEF, (2) knowing when to implement the short position on this stock, and (3) when to "cover" the short position. Steps 2 and 3 are relatively easy for the sophisticated investor who uses the Y-Process. This is because the Y-Process model signals the investor of the potential downturn/upturn in a timely fashion to allow a short/cover of the alias-stock.

• **Finding a high correlation alias-stock.** Most stock portfolios and mutual funds can be correlated to a stock exchange-traded fund. Many services provide this information free and most mutual funds contain correlation data (R^2) in their prospectus. Data can also be obtained by contacting the organization or broker directly. For funds that invest primarily in common stocks of foreign markets the fund will provide the correlation statistics upon request.

• **One more example of a market neutral position.** Suppose you own a large position in Singapore, an international mutual fund. When your Y-Process number has been violated indicating that your prospects for the Singapore market are dim, you could sell your fund, but if you're sitting on major gains in a taxable account, that sale would trigger a tax bill. Instead, you could hedge your exposure by shorting the Singapore WEBS fund—a proxy for the Singapore market—avoiding the big tax bill that would result in selling your long-held international fund shares. When the Y-Process signals an upward potential, you should cover your short position, pay a relatively small capital gain on that gain and maintain your long-term gains in your taxable Singapore account until you reach the fixed rate tax bracket.

Unfortunately, there is no free lunch. Why? Because you must pay short-term capital gain on any gain made on your short position. However, *you can have your cake and eat it too.* How? This requires a two step process. First, take the profits made on the short sale and buy additional shares of the stock. Next, at tax-time, sell a sufficient number of these "just bought shares" to pay the tax. Make sure to stipulate to your broker (in writing) before selling these shares that they *were last in and will be first out.* This total procedure assumes that the market returns to the upside. Why else would you cover your short position?

• **Conclusion.** The market-neutral strategy has two significant advantages: First, it gains time toward meeting your 18 months objective, and second, it pays the short term capital gain tax with short term capital gain money made on the short-sale. Unfortunately, this cake may be bittersweet. There is a possibility that the market will rise above the shorted value after you sold short and before you cover your short position. But, even in this case, the gain on your long-position offsets the loss on your short position *and* the IRS allows this as an investment tax-loss that reduces your income tax.

About the Author

Edward M. Yanis is the chairman and CEO of *Yanis Financial Services, Inc.* which provides a weekly newsletter containing market commentary as well as, buy, hold and sell recommendations on major market indexes. Mr. Yanis is the developer of the Y-Process, a revolutionary stock market model that forecasts crucial market turns enabling the investor to reduce risk and enhance returns.

Formerly, Mr. Yanis was the General Electric Company's Systems Engineering manager involved in the design, test and production of the AEGIS Combat System for the U.S. Navy AEGIS Cruisers, Ticonderoga class warships. He held that position for more than 20 years.

Prior to joining General Electric, Mr. Yanis taught applied electronics at the US Army Signal School for 2 years and after hours courses in Systems Engineering and Operations Analysis at the U.S. Department of Agriculture. He also took electrical engineering graduate courses for his Ph.D. in engineering at the American University, and Pennsylvania University.

Mr. Yanis holds a Bachelor of Electrical Engineering and a Master of Electrical Engineering from the Polytechnic University of New York. He also holds a Master of Business Administration in finance from Southern Illinois University. He is a member of the National Scholastic Honorary Society, Beta Gamma Sigma, the society for AACSB accredited business programs. He is also a registered Professional Engineer in New Jersey in addition to being a member of the American Society of Naval Engineers. Mr. Yanis is a past Vice Chairman of the International Electrical and Electronic Engineer committee on Reliability.

In 1970, Mr. Yanis invented the "Functional Flow Diagram and Descriptions," (F2D2) technique, an operations analysis methodology which defines, designs and verifies large-scale complex computer systems prior to implemention in hardware and software, thus providing large cost savings. The U.S. Government still uses this methodology and continues to teach system engineering courses based on the F2D2 approach. Using his expertise in both finance and systems engineering, Mr. Yanis solved the long standing, number one, concern facing warship designers of the United States Navy—*affordability*. Mr. Yanis used a revolutionary approach to develop a unique balance between system affordability and fighting capability for U.S. Navy warships. His mathematical model proved that properly networked computer systems would extend the useful life of a U. S. Navy frigate at only 17% of the cost of building a new frigate. He presented a technical paper on this subject to the *Royal Institute of Naval Architects* Conference in London, England, at their request, representing the General Electric Company. This paper was also submitted to the U. S. Navy for introduction into the fleet.

Mr. Yanis' technical career required extensive travel, e.g., Spain, Japan, Taiwan, and Israel, to support the Naval computer system designs for which he was in charge as a contractor officially representing the U. S. Navy.

His office is located in historic Cherry Hill, New Jersey where he resides with his wife and cofounder of *Yanis Financial Services, Inc.*, Judith.

Mr. Yanis' technical career required extensive travel, e.g., Spain, Japan, Taiwan, and Israel, to support the Naval computer system designs for which he was in charge as a contractor officially representing the U. S. Navy.

His office is located in historic Cherry Hill, New Jersey where he resides with his wife and cofounder of *Yanis Financial Services, Inc.*, Judith.

Glossary

A · B · C · D · E · F · G · H · I · J · K · L · M · N · O · P · Q · R · S · T · U · V · W · X · Y · Z

30-Day Average Yield. Based on yield to maturity of a fund's investments over a 30-day period and not on the dividends paid by the fund, which may differ.

Active Management. An investment approach that seeks to exceed the average returns of the financial markets. Active managers rely on research, market forecasts, and their own judgement and experience in selecting securities to buy or sell.

AMEX Major Market Index. An index of 20 blue chip industrial stocks that closely tracks the changes in the Dow Jones Industrial Average. Fifteen of the stocks in the index are also included in the Dow Jones Industrial Average.

Asked. Price that someone is willing to accept for a security or an asset. In the stock market, the ask portion of a stock quote is the lowest price

Asset Allocation Funds. Asset allocation funds have the ability to shift assets among asset classes (for example equities, bonds, and short-term instruments). Asset allocation funds take the concept of a private asset manager—a skilled professional who builds and manages a comprehensive portfolio for a client—and apply it to a mutual fund.

Asset-backed Securities. Bonds or notes backed by loan paper or accounts receivable originated by banks, credit card companies, or other providers of credit and often "enhanced" by a bank letter of credit or by insurance coverage provided by an institution other than the issuer.

Auction Market. A market for securities, typically found on a national securities exchange, in which trading in a particular security is conducted at a specific location with all qualified persons at that post able to bid or offer securities against orders via outcry.

Average Annual Total Return. Average annual total return is a hypothetical rate of return that, if achieved annually, would have produced the same cumulative total return if performance had been constant over the entire period. Average annual total returns smooth out variation in performance; they are not the same as actual year-by-year results.

Balloons. Final payments on a debt that are substantially larger than the preceding payments. Loans or mortgages are structured with payments when some projected event is expected to provide extra cash flow or when refinancing is anticipated. Balloon loans are sometimes called "partially amortized loans."

Basis Point. Smallest measure used in quoting yields on bonds and notes. One basis point is 0.01% of yield. For example, a bond's yield that changed from 12.72% to 12.52% has moved 20-basis points.

Bear market. When security prices decline 20% or more.

Bellwether Bond. For the U.S. market, it is the 30-year Treasury bond most recently offered by the government. Its performance is a benchmark for evaluating the bond market in general. Also called the long bond.

Beta. A measurement of a portfolio's sensitivity to market movements. It is a ratio of the portfolio's past price fluctuations compared to the fluctuations of a benchmark index, such as the S&P 500®. The S&P 500 has, as a generally accepted standard, a beta of 1.0. A beta less than 1.0 indicates that the fund's share price has fluctuated less (positively or negatively) than the S&P 500 for any given move in the index. The correlation measure R^2 should always be considered before beta to determine the validity of the comparison; a beta alone will not provide a complete picture of a fund's behavior. Beta can be calculated using the performance figures for any time period. For example, a mutual fund might calculate the beta based on 36 months returns. See **Volatility Measures.** See also **Correlation Measures,** R^2, and **S&P 500 Index.**

Bid. The price that someone is willing to pay for a security or an asset. In the stock market, the bid portion of a stock quote is the highest price anyone is willing to pay for a security at that time.

Bill (Treasury or T-Bill). A government security with a maturity of a year or less.

Blue-chip Stocks. Stocks of well-established companies that have had a history of earnings and dividend payments, as well as a reputation for sound management and quality products and services. Also known as large-cap stocks.

Broker. A person who gives advice and handles orders to buy or sell stocks, bonds, commodities and options.

Brokerage Firm. Financial-services firm that provide the service of buying and selling securities. Brokerage firms fall into two main camps, full-service brokers and discount brokers. Discount brokers charge far lower commissions than full service brokers and a growing number of deep discounters' charge especially low commissions. But there is a trade-off. If you use a discount broker, you will get little or no investment advice, so you must be willing to make your own buy and sell decisions. A full-service broker, on the other hand, will help you pick investments and devise a financial plan.

Bond. An interest-bearing promise to pay a specified sum of money principal amount—due on a specific date.

Bond Funds. Registered investment companies whose assets are invested in diversified portfolios of bonds.

Bull market. A time period when security prices increase greater than the previous all time high.

Call Feature. The terms of the bond contract giving the issuer the right or requiring the issuer to redeem or "call" all or a portion of an outstanding issue of bonds prior to their stated dates of maturity at a specified price, usually at or above par.

Call Protection. The aspects of the call provisions of an issue of callable securities which partially protect an investor against an issuer's call of the or act as a disincentive to the issuer's exercise of its call privileges. These features include restrictions on an issuer's right to call securities for a period of time after issuance (for example, an issue that cannot be called for ten years after its issuance is said to have ten years' call protection), or requirements that an issuer pay a premium redemption price for securities called within a certain period of time after issuance.

Callable Bond. A bond which the issuer is permitted or required to redeem before the stated maturity date at a specified price, usually at or above par, by giving notice of redemption in a manner specified in the bond contract.

Capital Appreciation. As the value of the securities in a portfolio increases, a fund's share price increases, meaning that the value of your investment rises. If you sell shares at a higher price than you paid for them do, you make a profit, or capital gain. If you sell shares at a lower price than paid for them, you'll have a capital loss. See also Dividends. See also Capital Gains.

Capital Gains. The difference between an asset's purchased price and selling price, when the asset was sold for more than it was bought. A capital loss is when the difference between the purchase price and the sale price of an asset was sold for less than it was bought

Capital Gain Distribution. Payment to mutual fund shareholders of gains realized during the year on securities that the fund has sold at a profit, minus any realized losses.

Capital Loss. Loss realized when an instrument or asset is sold at a price below its cost.

Capital Market. The market where capital funds, debt (bonds) and equity (stocks) are traded.

Cash Reserves. Cash deposits as well as short-term bank deposits, money market instruments, U. S. Treasury bills, bank certificates of deposit (CDs), repurchase agreements, commercial paper, and banker's acceptances.

Collateralized Mortgage Obligation (CMO). A mortgage-backed bond that separates mortgage pools into different maturity classes called tranches. This is accomplished by applying income (payments of principal and interest) from mortgages in the pool in the order the CMO's pay out.

Common Stock. A security presenting ownership rights in a corporation. A stockholder is entitled to share in the company's profits, some of which may be paid out as dividends. If the company does well, the value of each share generally goes up. Although common stocks have a history of long-term growth, their prices fluctuate based on changes in a company's financial condition and on overall market and economic conditions.

Compounding. Financial advisors love to talk about the magic of compounding. What magic? If your investments make 10% a year for five years, you earn not 50% but 61.1%. Here is the reason: as time goes on, you make money not only on your original investment but also on your accumulated gains from earlier years.

Convertible Bond. A corporate bond, usually a junior subordinated debenture that can be exchanged for shares of the issuer's common stock.

Correction. A reverse movement, usually downward, in the price of an individual stock, bond, commodity, index, or the stock markets as a whole.

Correlation Measures. Measures that show the validity of a comparison to an index based on the historical relationship between portfolio returns and index returns. See R^2. See also Volatility Measures.

Coupon. The term is used colloquially to refer to a security's interest rate.

Coupon Rate. The annual rate of interest payable on a debt security expressed as a percentage of the principal amount.

Coupon Yield (see Nominal Yield)

Credits. Loans, bonds, charge-account obligations, and open-account balances with commercial firms.

Cumulative Total Return. Cumulative total return reflects actual performance over a stated period of time.

Currency Risk. Risk that shifts in foreign exchange rates may undermine the value of overseas investments.

Current Income. Monies paid during the period an investment is held. Examples include bond interest and stock dividends.

Current Market Value. The amount a willing buyer will pay for a bond today, which may be at a premium (above face value) or a discount below face value).

Current Yield. The ratio of interest to the actual market price of the bond stated as a percentage: annual interest = current yield/ current market value.

CUSIP. An identification number assigned to each fund by the committee on Uniform Security Identification Procedures.

Cyclicals. Stocks of companies whose business prospects are tied to the economy. For example, steel companies often do poorly in a recession, when consumers are buying fewer large items such as cars and refrigerators.

DAX 100. The Deutscher Akteinindex (DAX) 100 is a market capitalization weighted index of the 100 most heavily traded stocks in the German market.

Denomination. The face amount or par value of a security which the issuer promises to pay on the maturity date.

Depression. A severe downturn in an economy that is marked by falling prices, reduced purchasing power, and high unemployment.

Discount. The difference between a bond's current market price and its face or redemption value.

Diversification. Diversification is the concept of spreading your money across different types of investments and/or issuers, thereby avoiding the risk that your portfolio will be badly bloodied because a single security or a particular market sector turns sour.

Dividends. Mutual fund dividends are paid out of income from the fund's investments. The tax on such dividends depends on whether the distributions resulted from interest income, or dividends received by the fund.

Dividend Income. Payment to shareholders of income from interest of dividends generated by a fund's investments.

Dollar Cost Averaging. With dollar-cost averaging, you invest a fixed amount on a regular basis—regardless of the current market trends. The investor buys more shares when the price is low and fewer shares when the price is high; the overall cost is lower than it would be if a constant number of shares were bought at set intervals. Dollar cost averaging does not assure a profit or protect against a loss in a declining market. You must continue to purchase shares both in market ups downs. The goal of dollar cost averaging is to attain a lower average cost per share.

Dow Jones Industrial Average (DJIA). Often referred to as the Dow, it is the best known and most widely reported indicator of the stock market's performance. The Dow tracks the price changes of 30 significant industrial stocks traded on the New York Stock Exchange. Their combined market value is equal to roughly 20% of the market value of all stocks listed on the New York Stock Exchange.

Duration. Duration estimates how much a bond's price fluctuates with changes in comparable interest rates. If rates rise 1.00%, for example, a fund with a 5-year duration is likely to lose about 5.00% of its value. Other factors also can influence a bond fund's performance and share price. A bond fund's actual performance may differ.

Expense Ratio. This figure tells you how much a mutual fund charges each year as a percentage of total fund assets. A fund with a 1.55% expense ratio, for instance, levies $1.55 for every $100 it has under management. Included in this figure are the fund's management fee, shareholder servicing costs, and any annual 12b-1 fee. A 12b-1 fee, which is named after the applicable Securities and Exchange Commission regulation, is levied to pay for the cost of attracting new investors to the fund. The fee may be used to buy advertising or to compensate brokers who sell the fund. See Management Fee.

Federal Home Mortgage Corporation (FHLMC or "Freddie Mac"). A federally created corporation established to facilitate the financing of single-family residential housing by creating and maintaining an active secondary market for conventional home mortgages.

Federal National Mortgage Association (FNMA or "Fannie Mae"). Government-sponsored private corporation authorized to purchase and sell mortgages and to otherwise facilitate the orderly operation of a secondary market for home mortgages.

FT-A-Nordic Index. The FT-Actuaries World Nordic Index is a market capitalization weighted index of over 90 stocks traded in four Scandinavian markets.

FT-All Shares. The FT-All Shares Index is a market capitalization weighted index of over 750 stocks traded in the U.K. market.

Fundamental analysis. Analysis technique that looks at a company's financial condition, management, and place in its industry to predict a company's stock price movement.

General Obligation Bond (GO). A municipal bond which is backed by the full faith and credit (taxing and borrowing power) of a municipality.

Government National Mortgage Association (GNMA or "Ginnie Mae"). An agency of the federal Department of Housing and Urban Development empowered to provide special assistance in financing home mortgages which is responsible for management and of federally owned mortgage portfolios. GNMA guarantees, with the full faith and credit of the U.S. Government, full and timely payment on mortgage-backed securities.

Graduated-Payment Mortgage (GPM). Mortgage featuring lower monthly payments at first, which steadily rise until they level off after a few years. GPMs, also known as "jeeps," are designed for young couples whose income is expected to grow as their career advance. A graduated-payment mortgage allows such a family to buy a house that would be unaffordable if payments started out at a high level. Persons planning to take on such a mortgage must be confident that their income will be able to keep pace with the rising payments.

Great Depression. The worldwide economic hard times generally regarded as having begun with the stock market collapse of Oct. 28-29, 1929 and continued through most of the 1930s.

Growth and Income Funds. Growth and income funds are designed to pursue long-term growth as well as regular dividend income. Some growth and income funds are weighted more heavily towards growth, others towards income.

Growth Funds. Growth funds are designed to pursue capital appreciation over the long-term. Some growth funds are broad-based, meaning that they have a wide range of stocks and industries in which they can invest. Others have a narrower focus—for example, they may invest in a particular type of stock, such as small-cap or cyclical stocks, or use a specialized approach to stock selection, such as investing only in stocks that are currently underpriced. Growth funds are more volatile than more conservative income or money market funds and generally reflect changes in market conditions and other company, political, and economic news.

Growth Stocks. Stocks of companies that have shown or are expected to show rapid earnings and revenue growth. Growth stocks are riskier than most other stocks and usually make little or no dividend payments to shareholders.

Hang Seng. The Hang Seng Index is a market capitalization weighted index of stocks of the 33 largest companies in the Hong Kong market.

Income/Distributions. For tax purposes, a mutual fund generally passes along dividends and interest it receives from securities it owns. A fund also passes along your share of the profits it makes when it sells securities for a higher price than it paid for them. You may choose to have these distributions sent to you or you may want to reinvest them. Distributions are subject to federal tax, and may also be subject to state or local taxes. Your distributions are taxable when they are, whether you take them in cash or reinvest them.

Index. An unmanaged group of securities whose overall performance is used as a standard to measure investment performance.

Indexing. Buying and holding a mix of stocks that match the performance of a broad stock-market barometer such as the Standard & Poor's 500 stock index.

Index Funds. Passively managed, limited-expense (advisor fee no higher than 0.50%) fund designed to replicate the performance of an unmanaged stock index on a reinvested basis.

Inflation Risk. The chance that the value of assets or income will be diminished as inflation shrinks the value of a currency.

Interest. The amount paid by a borrower as compensation for the use of borrowed money. This amount is generally expressed as an annual percentage of the principal amount.

Interest Rate. The annual rate expressed as a percentage of principal, payable for use of borrowed money.

International Funds. These funds invest in securities of countries outside the U.S. International funds can be global in scope or limited to a particular country or region, with the narrower-focused funds subject to increased volatility. Foreign investments, especially those in emerging markets, involve greater risks than those of U.S. investments do.

International Monetary Fund (IMF). An organization set up by the Bretton Woods Agreement in 1944. Unlike the World Bank, whose focus is on foreign exchange reserves and the balance of trade, the IMF focus is on lowering trade barriers and stabilizing currencies. While helping developing nations pay debts, the IMF usually imposes tough guidelines aimed at lowering inflation, cutting imports, and raising exports. IMF funds come mostly from the treasuries of industrialized nations.

Investment Advise. An organization that makes the day-to-day decisions regarding a portfolio's investments.

Investment Grade. The broad credit designation given bonds which have a high probability of being paid and minor, if any, speculative features. Bonds rated Baa and higher by Moody's Investors Service or BBB and higher by Standard & Poor's are deemed by those agencies to be "investment grade."

Investment Grade Bonds. Corporate and municipal bonds given one of the top four ratings by independent agencies. Issues rated BBB to AAA are considered investment grade.

Investment Objective. The identification of attributes associated with an investment or investment strategy, designed to isolate and compare risks, define acceptable levels of risk, and match investments with personal goals.

Issue Date. The date on which a security is deemed to be issued or originated.

Issuer. A state, political subdivision, agency or authority that borrows money through the sale of bonds or notes.

Junk Bond. A bond rated lower than Baa/BBB also called a "high-yield" bond. Junk bonds are speculative compared with investment grade bonds.

Lipper Funds Averages. Lipper Analytical Services, Inc., is a nationally recognized organization that reports on mutual fund total return performance and calculates fund rankings. Peer averages are based on universes of funds with the same investment objective. Peer group averages include reinvested dividends and capital gains, if any, and exclude sales charges.

Lipper Ranking. Fund ranking calculated quarterly or annually by Lipper Analytical Services of New York. Each fund is ranked within a universe of funds similar in investment objective. Lipper Analytical Services, Inc. is a nationally recognized organization that reports on mutual fund total return performance and calculates fund rankings.

Liquidity. The ability to buy or sell an asset quickly or the ability to convert to cash quickly.

Load funds. Mutual funds that charge a sales commission, as opposed to no-load funds, which do not levy a fee when you buy or sell. Some fund groups that sell directly to the public offer low-load funds, which charge an upfront fee of 2% or 3%, but most load funds are sold by brokers. To compensate brokers, load funds usually charge either a front-end sales commission when you buy the fund or a back-end sales commission when you sell. In addition, many broker-sold funds charge an annual 12b-1 fee, which is also used to compensate brokers. The 12b-1 fee is included in the fund's expense ratio.

"Long Bond." The 30-year bond is the longest maturity issued by the U.S. Treasury. It is also the most widely traded bond, not only in the United States but worldwide. Because it is such a key security, the most recently issued 30-year Treasury bond, known as the "long bond," is viewed as the benchmark against which all other bonds are measured.

Management Fee. Fee paid by a mutual fund to its investment manager or advisor for overseeing the portfolio. A management fee is usually between one-half and one percent of the fund's net asset value.

Market capitalization. The total market value of a company or stock. Market capitalization is calculated by multiplying the number of shares by the current market price of the shares.

Market Risk. The risk that the price of a security will rise or fall due to changing economic, political, or market conditions, or due to a company's individual situation.

Marketability. The ease or difficulty with which securities can be sold in the market.

Market Timing. Shifting money in and out of investment markets in an effort to take advantage of rising prices and avoid being stung by downturns. Few, if any, investors manage to be consistently successful in timing markets.

Maturity or Maturity Date. The date upon which the principal of a security becomes due and payable to the security holder.

Maturity Value. The amount (other than periodic interest payment) that will be received at the time a security is redeemed at its maturity. On most securities the maturity value equals the par value.

Mid-cap Stocks. An investment categorization based on the market capitalization of a company.

Mortgage-Backed Securities (MBS). Securities backed by mortgages. Such certificates are issued by the Federal Home Loan Mortagage Corporation, and the Federal National Mortgage Association. Others are guaranteed by the Government National Mortgage Association. Investors receive payments out of the interest and principle on the underlying mortgages. Sometimes banks issue certificates backed by conventional mortgages, selling them to large institutional investors. The growth of mortgage-backed certificates and the secondary mortgage market in which they are traded has helped keep mortgage money available for home financing.

Moving Averages. The average price of a mutual fund calculated periodically over some designated period of time. For example, to calculate a 13-week average, total the weekly closing prices for 13 weeks and divide by 13. The average price is plotted on a chart against actual prices. The effect of a moving average is to minimize short-term price fluctuations and highlight long-term price fluctuations.

MSCI Emerging Markets Free Index. The Morgan Stanley Capital International Emerging Markets Free Index is a market capitalization weighted index of over 850 stocks traded in 22 world markets.

MSCI EAFE Index. The Morgan Stanley Capital International Europe, Australasia, Far East Index is an unmanaged index of over 1,000 foreign stocks. The index may be compiled in two ways: a market capitalization weighted (cap-weighted) version and a gross domestic product weighted (GDP-weighted) version.

MSCI Europe Index. The Morgan Stanley Capital International Europe Index is a market capitalization weighted index of over 550 stocks traded in 14 European markets.

MSCI Far East ex-Japan Free Index. The Morgan Stanley Capital International Combined Far East ex Free Index is a market capitalization weighted index of over 450 stocks traded in eight Asian markets, excluding Japan.

MSCI France Index. Also known as the Morgan Stanley Capital International France Index. It is an unmanaged index of over 75 foreign stock prices, and reflects the common stock prices of the index companies translated into U.S. dollars, assuming reinvestment of all dividends paid by the index stocks net of any applicable foreign taxes.

MSCI Germany Index. Also known as the Morgan Stanley Capital International Germany Index. It is an unmanaged index of over 75 foreign stock prices, and reflects the common stock prices of the index companies translated into U.S. dollars, assuming reinvestment of all dividends paid by the index stocks net of any applicable foreign taxes.

MSCI Hong Kong Index. Also known as the Morgan Stanley Capital International Hong Kong Index. It is an unmanaged index of over 38 foreign stock prices, and reflects the common stock prices of the index companies translated into U.S. dollars, assuming reinvestment of all dividends paid by the index stocks net of any applicable foreign taxes.

MSCI Japan Index. Also known as the Morgan Stanley Capital International Japan Index. It is an unmanaged index of over 317 foreign stock prices, and reflects the common stock prices of the index companies translated into U.S. dollars, assuming reinvestment of all dividends paid by the index stocks net of any applicable foreign taxes.

MSCI Emerging Markets Free—Latin America Index. Morgan Stanley Capital International emerging Markets Free -Latin America index is a market capitalization weighted index of approximately 170 stocks traded in seven Latin American markets.

MSCI Nordic Countries Free Index. Known as the Morgan Stanley Capital International Nordic Countries Index. It is an unmanaged index of over 95 foreign stock prices, and reflects the common stock prices of the index companies translated into U.S. dollars, assuming reinvestment of all dividends paid by the index stocks net of any applicable foreign taxes.

MSCI Pacific Index. The Morgan Stanley Capital International Pacific Index is a market capitalization weighted index of over 400 stocks traded in six Pacific-region markets.

MSCI United Kingdom Index. Also known as the Morgan Stanley Capital International United Kingdom Index. It is an unmanaged index of over 143 foreign stock prices, and reflects the common stock prices of the index companies translated into U.S. dollars, assuming reinvestment of all dividends paid by the index stocks net of any applicable foreign taxes.

MSCI World Index. Morgan Stanley Capital International World Index is a market capitalization weighted equity index of over 1,500 stocks traded in 22 world markets.

Municipal Securities. A general term referring to securities issued by local governmental such as cities, towns, villages, counties or special districts, as well as securities issued by states and political or agencies of states. A prime feature of these securities is that interest on them is generally exempt from federal income taxes and, in some cases, state and local taxes too.

Mutual Fund. A fund that pools the money of its investors to buy a variety of securities. Open-end mutual funds sell as many shares as investors want. Closed-end mutual funds offer only a fixed number of shares and usually trade on an exchange. A professional manager invests the group's money.

Nasdaq. An electronic stock market run by the National Association of Securities Dealers. Brokers get price quotes through a computer network and trade via telephone or computer network.

Nasdaq Composite Index. An unmanaged index of over-the-counter stock prices that does not assume the reinvestment of dividends.

NAV Change. The difference between today's closing net asset value (NAV) and previous day's closing net asset value (NAV).

NAV Change %. The percentage change between today's closing net asset value NAV) and the previous day's closing net asset value (NAV).

Net Asset Value (NAV). The dollar value of one share of a fund determined by taking the total assets of a fund, subtracting the total liabilities, and dividing by the total number of shares outstanding.

Net Yield. Rate of return on a security net of out-of-pocket costs associated with its purchase, such as commissions or markups.

Nikkei Stock Average. An index of 225 leading stocks traded on the Tokyo stock exchange.

Nominal Yield (Coupon Yield). The stated interest rate paid on a bond, computed by dividing the amount of annual income by the bond's par value.

Note. A debt obligation similar to a bond, but with a maturity date less than five years from date of issue.

Offer Price. The lowest price that a seller is willing to accept from a prospective buyer. In the case of a mutual fund with a sales charge, this price is the net asset value (NAV) plus the sales charge. In the case of no-load funds, it is the NAV.

Offering Date. The date on which a distribution of stocks or bonds will first be to the public.

Opportunity Cost. The cost of doing one thing and not another. Example: Not investing present dollars always involves a cost, i.e., the loss of an opportunity to earn a realistic return on these dollars. See "**Present Value.**"

Opportunity Risk. The risk that a better opportunity may present itself after you have already committed your money elsewhere.

Paper. Any short-term debt security.

Par. The nominal or face value of a security as given on the certificate or instrument. The par value is the amount on which interest payments calculated.

Passive management. A low-cost investment strategy in which a mutual fund attempts to match—rather than outperform—a particular stock or bond market index. Also known as indexing.

Portfolio. A collection of securities held by an investor.

Portfolio Diversification. Holding a variety of securities so that a portfolio's return is not hurt by the poor performance of a single security or industry.

Premium. The amount by which a bond sells above its par (face) value.

Present Value. The value at the current time of a cash payment which is expected to be received in the future, discounted to reflect the fact that an amount received today could be invested to earn interest for the period to the future date.

Price/Earnings (P/E) Ratio. A ratio to evaluate a stock's worth. It is calculated by dividing the stock's price by an earnings-per-share figure. If calculated with the past year's earnings, it is called the trailing P/E. If calculated with an analyst's forecast for next year's earnings, it is called a forward P/E. Also called the P/E ratio or multiple. A stock selling for $20, with earnings of $2 per share, has a price/earnings ration of 10.

Principal. The amount of your own money you put into an investment.

Primary Market (New Issue Market). The market on which newly issued securities are sold, including government security auctions and underwriting purchases of blocks of new issues, which are then resold.

Quant. Slang reference to an analyst who uses quantitative research techniques.

Quantitative Funds. Mutual funds whose portfolio management decisions are based on quantitative analysis, which is usually developed using computerized statistical models of market behavior.

R^2. A measurement of how closely the portfolio's performance with the performance of other benchmark indexes, such as the S&P 500. R^2 is a proportion which ranges between 0.00 and 1.0. An R^2 of 1.00 indicates perfect correlation to the benchmark index, that is, all of the portfolio's fluctuations are explained by performance fluctuations of the index, while an R^2 of 0.00 indicates no correlation. Therefore, the lower the R^2, the more the fund's performance is affected by factors other than the market as measured by that benchmark index. See Correlation Measures. See also Volatility Measures, Beta, and S&P 500 Index.

Ratings. Designations used by investors' services to give relative indications credit quality.

Redemption. The paying off or buying back of a bond by the issuer.

Refunding. The replacement of a bond issue by a new bond issue at conditions generally more favorable to the issuer.

Revenue Bond. A municipal bond payable solely from net or gross non-tax revenues derived from tolls, charges or rents paid by users of the facility

Redemption Fee. A fee you pay when you redeem, or sell, your shares. Not all funds charge redemption fees.

Relative Strength. The price movement of a stock compared with the movement of an index, market or industry sector.

Relative Volatility. A ratio of a portfolio's standard deviation to the standard deviation of a benchmark index. See Volatility Measures.

Return per Unit of Risk. A ratio that compares the average annual total return of a fund to the average standard deviation of those returns over a historical-month period. Return Per Unit of Risk (RUR) attempts to show the relationship between the fund's historical return and the amount of risk associated with the generation of that return. For example, a RUR of 1.00 means that for every percentage point of volatility (annualized standard deviation) there has been one percentage point of return. See Volatility Measures.

Risk. Anything that causes your investment to behave differently from what you expect. The Y-Process risk is by the percent of the time you are in of the stock market an not in the money market.

Russell 1000® Index. The Russell 1000® Index consists of the largest 1000 companies in the Russell 3000® Index. This index represents the universe of large stocks from which most active money managers select. The Index was developed with a base value of 130.00 as of December 31, 1986.

Russell 2000® Index. The Russell 2000® Index is an unmanaged index of 2,000 small capitalization stocks.

Sales Charge. Fee on the purchase of new shares of a mutual fund. A sales charge is similar to paying a premium for a security in that the customer must pay a higher offering price. Sometimes called a load.

Salomon Brothers GNMA Index. The Salomon Brothers GNMA Index is a market capitalization weighted index of 15- and 30-year fixed-rate securities backed by mortgage pools of the Government National Mortgage Association (GNMA).

Secondary Market. The market for securities previously offered or sold.

Sector Funds. Mutual funds that invest in a single-industry sector, such as, regional banks, health care, chemicals, or retailing. These funds tend to be more volatile than funds holding a diversified portfolio of stocks in many industries.

Security. Generally, an instrument evidencing debt of or equity in a common enterprise in which a person invests on the expectation of financial profits. The term includes notes, stocks, bonds, debentures or other forms of negotiable and non-negotiable evidences of indebtedness or ownership.

Share Price. The value of one share in the fund. With most funds, the share price is calculated every day, because the value of a fund's securities changes every day in response to the movements of the stock, bond and money markets. For some funds, share price is calculated on an hourly basis.

Shareholder. The owner of one or more shares of stock in a corporation or one or more shares or units of a mutual fund. Shareholder rights can vary according to the articles of incorporation of the by-laws of a particular company.

Short Covering. Trades that reverse, or close out, short-sale positions. In the stock market, for instance, shares are purchased to replace the shares previously borrowed.

Short Interest. Total number of shares of a given stock that have been sold short and not yet repurchased.

Short Selling. A trading strategy that anticipates a drop in a share's price. Stock or another financial instrument is borrowed from a broker and then sold, creating a short position. That position is reversed, or covered, when the stock is repurchased to repay the loan. The short seller profits if they're able to repurchase stock at a lower price than they would receive in creating the short position.

Small-capitalization Stocks. Shares of relatively small publicly traded corporations, typically with a total market value, or capitalization, of less than $600 million. Also called small-cap stocks or small caps.

Standard & Poor's Midcap 400 Index (S&P 400). The Standard & Poor's Mid Cap 400 Index is a widely recognized unmanaged index of 400 medium-capitalization stocks.

Standard & Poor's 500 Index (S&P 500).® A benchmark index of 500 large stocks maintained by Standard & Poor's, a division of McGraw-Hill Co. The S&P 500 is a widely recognized, unmanaged index of common stocks.

Standard Deviation. A statistical measure of the historical volatility of a portfolio. Standard deviation measures the dispersion of a fund's periodic returns (often based on 36 months of returns). The wider the dispersions, the larger the standard deviation. This is an independent measure of volatility; it is not relative to an index.

Stop Order. An investor's order to a broker to buy or sell a security when its market price reaches a certain level.

Taxable Equivalent Yield. Interest rate that must be received on a taxable security to provide the holder the same after-tax return as that earned on a tax-exempt security.

Technicals. Short-term trends that technical analysts can sometimes identify as significant in the price movement of a security or a commodity. Such trends may be in the demand and supply for securities, options, mutual funds, and commodities based on trading volume and price studies. Technical analysis is generally not concerned with the financial position of a company.

Term. The time during which interest payments will be made on a bond or certificate of deposit.

TOPIX. The Tokyo Stock Exchange Index (TOPIX) is a market capitalization weighted index of over 1,100 stocks traded in the Japanese market.

Total Return. A percentage change, over a specified time period, in a mutual fund's net asset value, with the ending net asset value adjusted to account for the reinvestment of all distributions of dividends and capital gains. Return on an investment, takes into account capital appreciation, dividends or interest, and individual tax considerations adjusted for present value and expressed on an annual basis.

Trading Symbol. An abbreviation for stock and/or fund names for use with automated brokerage trading and quote service. Can also be used by Quotron and other electronic information systems for access to fund performance data.

TSE 300. The Toronto Stock Exchange (TSE) 300 is a market capitalization weighted index of 300 stocks traded in the Canadian market.

Turnover Rate. A measure of the fund's trading activity calculated by dividing total purchases or sales of portfolio securities (whichever is lower) by the fund's net assets.

Underwrite. To purchase a bond or note from the issuing body to resell it to the general public.

Unit Investment Trust (UIT). An SEC registered Investment Company that invests in a portfolio of securities on behalf of investors who share a common objective. Investors receive periodic interest and, upon maturity, redemption value. The UIT is not actively managed.

Value Investing. Value investors are the stock market's bargain hunters. They often lean toward beaten-down companies whose shares appear cheap when compared to current earnings or corporate assets. Value investors typically buy stocks with high dividend yields, or ones that trade at a low price-to-earnings ratio or low price-to-book-value. The value investment style often is contrasted with the growth style. The two styles tend to take turns being popular on Wall Street. One-year growth stocks will be all the rage; the next year value stocks may dominate.

Value Stocks. Stocks that are considered to be undervalued, either according to their book value or their current or projected earnings. These stocks can be those of smaller less well known companies and may be more volatile than those of larger companies.

Volatility. The fluctuations in value of a mutual fund or other security. The greater a fund's volatility, the wider the fluctuations between its high and low prices in a short-term period.

Volatility Measures. Volatility measures seek to compare a portfolio's relative share price fluctuations or total returns to those of a relevant market, represented by the benchmark index. Measures of volatility are based on historical performance; they are not calculated for funds that are less than three years old. See Beta, Relative Volatility, and Return per Unit or Risk. See also Correlation Measures.

Wilshire 5000 Stock Index. Broadest index covering Nasdaq Stock Market stocks and all stocks traded on all the New York Stock Exchange and American Stock Exchange. It is a market value weighted index.

Yankee Bonds (Yankee Credits). Dollar-denominated bonds issued in the U.S. by foreign banks and corporations.

Yield. Current income (interest or dividends) earned by an investment, expressed as a percentage of the investment's price. The percentage of return an investor receives based on the amount invested or on the current market value of holdings.

Yield Curve. The relationship at a given point in time between yields on a group of fixed-income securities with varying maturities—commonly, Treasury bills, notes, and bonds. The curve typically slopes upward since longer maturities normally have higher yields, although it can be flat or even inverted.

Yield to Call. Yield on a bond assuming the bond will be redeemed by the issuer at the first call date specified.

Yield To Maturity. Used to determine the rate of return an investor will receive if a long-term, interest-bearing investment, such as a bond is held to its maturity date. It takes into account purchase price, redemption value, time to maturity, coupon yield and the time between interest payments.

Y-Process. A model founded on two concepts. The first, the law of supply and demand and the second, that stock prices tend to move in trends. The model uses an exponential moving average with a smoothing constant of .1177.

YTD. Stands for Year To Date. Used in mutual fund tables to indicate the rate of return of the fund from the beginning of the year to the present date.

Zero-Coupon Bond. A bond where no periodic interest payments are made. The investor purchases the bond at a discounted price and receives one payment at maturity. The maturity value an investor receives is equal to the principal invested plus interest earned compounded semiannually at the original rate to maturity. Interest income from zero-coupon bonds is subject to taxes annually even though no payments will be made.

A · B · C · D · E · F · G · H · I · J · K · L · M · N · O · P · Q · R · S · T · U · V · W · X · Y · Z

Appendix A. S&P 500 Index for 1940

Date - (Friday)	S&P500 Index Price	Y-Process Number	Risk Index (RI)	Ypro buy (B) or sell (S)	Y-Process values	Annual Return (AR)*	Annual Total Return (ATR)**	Year	S&P500 Index ATR % (Bahf)	Y-Process ATR % (Ypro)
1/2/1940	12.63	12.49	1.11%	S0	12.63					
1/5/1940	12.66	12.51	1.17%	'B1'	12.64	rate= 0.12%		40	-8.95%	8.63%
1/12/1940	12.13	12.47	-2.78%	S1				41	-9.67%	7.60%
1/19/1940	12.15	12.43	-2.32%					42	18.42%	23.89%
1/26/1940	12.15	12.40	-2.05%					43	24.70%	29.37%
2/2/1940	12.06	12.36	-2.50%	S1'		RoR/t-bill= 0.00%		44	18.63%	79.70%
2/9/1940	12.37	12.36	0.05%	'B2'	12.36	rate= 2.52%	ATR ? ATR	45	34.53%	32.22%
2/16/1940	12.29	12.36	-0.54%	S2		1940 AR= -15.29%	-8.95% 6.34%	46	-7.26%	9.84%
2/23/1940	12.23	12.34	-0.92%		1940 Y-Proc AR= 6.80%	8.63% 1.83%	47	5.52%	9.38%
3/1/1940	12.06	12.31	-2.08%		1940 T-Bill= 0.01%	Mkt Risk= 28.85%	48	5.49%	15.45%
3/8/1940	12.20	12.30	-0.81%		Div= 6.34%	Rnd Turns=4.5	49	17.05%	21.63%
3/15/1940	12.07	12.27	-1.68%						Mkt Risk	Rnd Turns
3/22/1940	12.13	12.26	-1.05%					40	28.85%	Rnd Turns=4.5
3/29/1940	12.18	12.25	-0.57%	S2'	RoR/t-bill= 0.00%			41	30.77%	Rnd Turns=2.5
4/5/1940	12.48	12.28	1.62%	B3	12.26			42	59.62%	Rnd Turns=.50
4/12/1940	12.32	12.28	0.29%	B3'	12.28	rate= 0.19%		43	63.46%	Rnd Turns=4.0
4/19/1940	12.04	12.26	-1.80%	S3				44	84.62%	Rnd Turns=5.0
4/26/1940	12.08	12.24	-1.30%					45	90.38%	Rnd Turns=3.0
5/3/1940	12.12	12.22	-0.86%					46	42.31%	Rnd Turns=2.5
5/10/1940	11.76	12.17	-3.49%					47	38.46%	Rnd Turns=4.0
5/17/1940	9.95	11.91	-19.71%					48	48.08%	Rnd Turns=4.5
5/24/1940	9.16	11.59	-26.51%					49	51.92%	Rnd Turns=1.0
5/31/1940	9.27	11.32	-22.08%							
6/7/1940	9.34	11.08	-18.68%							
6/14/1940	9.94	10.95	-10.17%			AVE ROUND TURNS FOR 40s =				
6/21/1940	9.91	10.83	-9.28%							
6/28/1940	9.98	10.73	-7.52%							
7/5/1940	9.94	10.64	-7.03%							
7/12/1940	9.95	10.56	-6.12%							
7/19/1940	9.97	10.49	-5.22%							
7/26/1940	9.97	10.43	-4.62%							
8/2/1940	10.25	10.41	-1.56%							
8/9/1940	10.27	10.39	-1.21%							
8/16/1940	9.84	10.33	-4.98%							
8/23/1940	10.19	10.31	-1.23%	S3'	RoR/t-bill= 0.01%					
8/30/1940	10.50	10.34	1.54%	B4	10.33					
9/6/1940	10.85	10.40	4.16%	B4'	10.39	rate= 0.65%				
9/13/1940	10.31	10.39	-0.77%	'S4'	RoR/t-bill= 0.00%					
9/20/1940	10.59	10.41	1.66%	B5	10.40					
9/27/1940	10.58	10.43	1.37%							

10/4/1940	10.78	10.48	2.82%			
10/11/1940	10.58	10.49	0.85%			
10/18/1940	10.72	10.52	1.89%			
10/25/1940	10.73	10.54	1.73%			
11/1/1940	11.08	10.61	4.26%			
11/8/1940	11.23	10.68	4.88%			
11/15/1940	11.17	10.74	3.84%			
11/22/1940	10.79	10.75	0.39%	B5'	10.74	rate= 3.32%
11/29/1940	10.57	10.73	-1.49%	S5		
12/6/1940	10.53	10.71	-1.67%			
12/13/1940	10.69	10.70	-0.14%			
12/20/1940	10.41	10.67	-2.51%			
12/27/1940	10.44	10.65	-1.96%			
12/31/1940	10.58	10.64	-0.55%	S5'	RoR/t-bill= 0.00%	10.58

Appendix B. S&P 500 Index for 1950

Date - (Friday)	S&P500 Index Price	Y-Process Number	Risk Index (RI)	Ypro buy (B) or sell (S)	Y-Process values	Annual Return (AR)*	Annual Total Return (ATR)**
1/3/1950	16.66	16.21	2.69%	B0			ATR ? ATR
1/6/1950	16.98	16.30	3.98%		1950 AR= 21.78%	28.98%	7.20%
1/13/1950	16.67	16.35	1.93%		1950 Y-Proc AR= 22.64%	28.87%	6.23%
1/20/1950	16.90	16.41	2.87%		1950 T-Bill= 1.22%	Mkt Risk= 86.54%	
1/27/1950	16.82	16.46	2.11%		Div= 7.20%	Rnd Turns=2.0	
2/3/1950	17.29	16.56	4.20%				
2/10/1950	17.24	16.64	3.45%				
2/17/1950	17.15	16.71	2.59%				
2/24/1950	17.28	16.77	2.92%				
3/3/1950	17.29	16.84	2.62%				
3/10/1950	17.09	16.87	1.30%				
3/17/1950	17.45	16.94	2.93%				
3/24/1950	17.56	17.01	3.11%				
3/31/1950	17.29	17.05	1.40%				
4/7/1950	17.82	17.14	3.81%				
4/14/1950	17.96	17.24	4.02%				
4/21/1950	17.96	17.33	3.53%				
4/28/1950	17.96	17.40	3.11%				
5/5/1950	18.22	17.50	3.95%				
5/12/1950	18.18	17.58	3.29%				
5/19/1950	18.68	17.71	5.18%				
5/26/1950	18.67	17.83	4.52%				
6/2/1950	18.79	17.94	4.51%				
6/9/1950	19.26	18.10	6.03%				
6/16/1950	18.97	18.20	4.04%				
6/23/1950	19.14	18.32	4.31%	B0' 18.30	rate= 9.19%		
6/30/1950	17.69	18.24	-3.13%	S1			
7/7/1950	17.67	18.18	-2.87%				
7/14/1950	16.87	18.03	-6.85%				
7/21/1950	17.59	17.98	-2.20%				
7/28/1950	17.69	17.94	-1.44%	S1'	RoR/t-bill= 0.14%		
8/4/1950	18.14	17.97	0.94%	B1 17.96			
8/11/1950	18.28	18.01	1.49%				
8/18/1950	18.68	18.09	3.17%				
8/25/1950	18.54	18.14	2.14%				
9/1/1950	18.55	18.19	1.92%				
9/8/1950	18.75	18.26	2.61%				
9/15/1950	19.29	18.38	4.70%				
9/22/1950	19.44	18.51	4.79%				
9/29/1950	19.45	18.62	4.26%				

Year	S&P500 Index ATR % (Bahf)	Y-Process ATR %	(Ypro)
			1.290
50	28.98%	28.87%	1.224
51	22.39%	23.81%	1.171
52	17.07%	17.93%	0.992
53	-0.78%	5.32%	1.493
54	49.30%	48.49%	1.300
55	30.61%	32.11%	1.064
56	6.35%	13.72%	0.902
57	-9.83%	10.36%	1.412
58	41.23%	37.26%	1.115
59	11.54%	13.78%	0.000
	Mkt Risk	Rnd Turns	0.865
50	86.54%	Rnd Turns=2.0	0.750
51	75.00%	Rnd Turns=3.0	0.731
52	73.08%	Rnd Turns=4.0	0.500
53	50.00%	Rnd Turns=3.0	1.000
54	100.00%	Rnd Turns=0.0	0.942
55	94.23%	Rnd Turns=2.0	0.519
56	51.92%	Rnd Turns=5.0	0.404
57	40.38%	Rnd Turns=1.5	0.865
58	86.54%	Rnd Turns=2.0	
59	76.92%	Rnd Turns=1.0	

AVE ROUND TURNS FOR 50s =   2.35

10/6/1950	20.12	18.80	6.56%				
########	19.85	18.93	4.66%				
########	19.96	19.05	4.56%				
########	19.77	19.14	3.21%				
11/3/1950	19.85	19.22	3.16%				
########	19.94	19.31	3.17%				
########	19.86	19.38	2.44%				
########	20.32	19.49	4.09%				
12/1/1950	19.66	19.51	0.76%	B1'	19.50	rate=	8.59%
12/8/1950	19.40	19.50	-0.51%	S2			
########	19.33	19.48	-0.78%	S2'		RoR/t-bill=	0.07%
########	20.07	19.55	2.58%	B3	19.50		
########	20.43	19.66	3.78%				
########	20.41	19.66	3.78%	B3'	20.41	rate=	4.65%

Appendix C. S&P 500 Index for 1960

Date - (Friday)	S&P500 Index Price	Y-Process Number	Risk Index (RI)	Ypro buy (B) or sell (S)	Y-Process values	Annual Return (AR)*	Annual Total Return (ATR)**	Year	S&P500 Index ATR % (Bahf)	Y-Process ATR % (Ypro)
1/1/1960	59.91	58.35	2.60%	B0				60	0.38%	9.49%
1/8/1960	59.50	58.49	1.69%	B0'	58.49 rate= -0.023			61	25.95%	24.65%
1/15/1960	58.38	58.49	-0.18%	S1				62	8.43%	14.02%
1/22/1960	57.38	58.36	-1.71%		1960 AR= -2.972%			63	21.93%	21.50%
1/29/1960	55.61	58.04	-4.38%		1960 FIRM AR= 8.005%			64	15.92%	15.73%
2/5/1960	55.98	57.81	-3.26%		1960 T-Bill= 2.930%			65	12.00%	14.36%
2/12/1960	55.46	57.54	-3.74%		Div= 3.35%			66	-9.52%	6.17%
2/19/1960	56.24	57.39	-2.04%					67	23.12%	24.44%
2/26/1960	56.16	57.25	-1.94%					68	10.62%	17.23%
3/4/1960	54.47	56.93	-4.52%					69	-7.93%	9.38%
3/11/1960	54.24	56.62	-4.39%						Mkt Risk	Rnd Turns
3/18/1960	55.01	56.43	-2.59%					60	44.23%	Rnd Turns=5.0
3/25/1960	55.98	56.39	-0.73%					61	92.31%	Rnd Turns=3.0
4/1/1960	55.43	56.28	-1.53%	S1'	RoR/t-bill= 0.0068			62	40.38%	Rnd Turns=2.0
4/8/1960	56.39	56.30	0.16%	B1	56.30			63	92.31%	Rnd Turns=1.0
4/15/1960	56.43	56.32	0.20%	B1'	56.31 rate= 0.0002			64	92.31%	Rnd Turns=2.0
4/22/1960	55.42	56.22	-1.44%	S2				65	78.85%	Rnd Turns=2.0
4/29/1960	54.37	56.01	-3.01%					66	32.26%	Rnd Turns=3.5
5/6/1960	54.75	55.86	-2.04%					67	86.54%	Rnd Turns=3.5
5/13/1960	55.30	55.80	-0.91%	S2'	RoR/t-bill= 0.0028			68	73.08%	Rnd Turns=3.5
5/20/1960	55.83	55.81	0.03%	B2'	55.81 rate= 0.0093			69	23.08%	Rnd Turns=3.5
5/27/1960	55.74	55.81	-0.13%	S2'	RoR/t-bill= 0.0011					
6/3/1960	56.23	55.86	0.65%	B3	55.82					
6/10/1960	57.97	56.12	3.19%			AVE ROUND TURNS FOR 60s=2.9				
6/17/1960	57.44	56.28	2.02%							
6/24/1960	57.68	56.45	2.13%							
7/1/1960	57.06	56.53	0.93%							
7/8/1960	57.38	56.63	1.30%	B3'	56.60 rate= 0.0141					
7/15/1960	56.05	56.57	-0.93%	S3						
7/22/1960	54.72	56.36	-2.99%							
7/29/1960	55.51	56.26	-1.36%							
8/5/1960	55.44	56.17	-1.32%	S3'	RoR/t-bill= 0.0028					
8/12/1960	56.66	56.24	0.75%	B4	56.22					
8/19/1960	57.01	56.33	1.19%							
8/26/1960	57.60	56.49	1.93%							
9/2/1960	57.00	56.55	0.78%	B4'	56.53 rate= 0.0056					
9/9/1960	56.11	56.51	-0.71%	S4						
9/16/1960	55.11	56.35	-2.25%							
9/23/1960	53.90	56.07	-4.02%							
9/30/1960	53.52	55.77	-4.21%							

Center annotation box (Annual Total Return):

	ATR	? ATR
	0.378%	3.35%
	9.49%	1.48%
Mkt Risk=44.23%		
Rnd Turns=5.0		

10/7/1960	54.03	55.57	-2.85%			
########	54.88	55.50	-1.12%			
########	53.32	55.25	-3.61%			
########	53.41	55.04	-3.04%			
11/4/1960	54.90	55.02	-0.23%	S4'		RoR/t-bill= 0.0051
########	55.87	55.13	1.33%	B5	55.04	
########	55.82	55.22	1.08%			
########	56.13	55.33	1.43%			
12/2/1960	55.39	55.34	0.09%			
12/9/1960	56.65	55.50	2.03%			
########	57.20	55.71	2.61%			
########	57.44	55.92	2.65%			
########	58.11	56.18	3.32%	B5'	58.11	rate= 0.056

Dancing With Bears

Appendix D. S&P 500 Index for 1970

Date - (Friday)	S&P500 Index Price	Y-Process Number	Risk Index (RI)	Ypro buy (B) or sell (S)	Y-Process values	Annual Return (AR)*	Annual Total Return (ATR)**	Year	S&P500 Index ATR % (Bahf)	Y-Process ATR % (Ypro)
1/2/1970	93.00	94.05	-1.13%	SO'			ATR ? ATR	70	3.51%	23.25%
1/9/1970	92.40	93.87	-1.59%		1970 AR= 0.10%	3.51%	3.41%	71	13.80%	19.59%
1/16/1970	90.92	93.53	-2.87%		1970 FIRM 21.94%	23.25%	1.31%	72	18.30%	20.15%
					AR=					
1/23/1970	89.07	93.01	-4.43%		1970 T-Bill= 6.46%	Mkt Risk=38.46%		73	-13.91%	7.84%
1/30/1970	85.02	92.08	-8.31%		Div= 3.41%	Rnd Turns=0.5		74	-24.47%	13.35%
2/6/1970	86.33	91.41	-5.89%					75	35.63%	41.63%
2/13/1970	86.54	90.85	-4.98%					76	22.92%	13.40%
2/20/1970	88.03	90.53	-2.84%					77	-6.59%	9.27%
2/27/1970	89.50	90.41	-1.02%					78	6.34%	19.94%
3/6/1970	89.44	90.31	-0.97%					79	15.02%	21.16%
3/13/1970	87.86	90.03	-2.47%						Mkt Risk	Rnd Turns
3/20/1970	87.06	89.69	-3.02%					70	38.46%	Rnd Turns=0.5
3/27/1970	89.92	89.73	0.22%					71	65.38%	Rnd Turns=5.0
4/3/1970	89.39	89.69	-0.34%					72	80.77%	Rnd Turns=6.5
4/10/1970	88.24	89.53	-1.46%					73	30.77%	Rnd Turns=2.5
4/17/1970	85.67	89.09	-3.99%					74	11.44%	Rnd Turns=3.0
4/24/1970	82.77	88.35	-6.74%					75	75.00%	Rnd Turns=2.5
5/1/1970	81.44	87.55	-7.50%					76	78.85%	Rnd Turns=3.0
5/8/1970	79.44	86.60	-9.02%					77	19.23%	Rnd Turns=3.5
5/15/1970	76.90	85.47	-11.14%					78	48.08%	Rnd Turns=2.0
5/22/1970	77.25	84.51	-9.40%					79	71.15%	Rnd Turns=3.5
5/29/1970	76.55	83.58	-9.19%							
6/5/1970	76.17	82.72	-8.60%			AVE ROUND TURNS FOR FOR 70s=	3.65			
6/12/1970	74.21	81.72	-10.13%							
6/19/1970	77.05	81.18	-5.36%							
6/26/1970	73.47	80.28	-9.27%							
7/3/1970	72.92	79.42	-8.92%							
7/10/1970	74.57	78.86	-5.75%							
7/17/1970	77.69	78.73	-1.34%							
7/24/1970	77.82	78.63	-1.04%							
7/31/1970	78.05	78.57	-0.67%							
8/7/1970	77.28	78.43	-1.48%							
8/14/1970	75.18	78.05	-3.82%	SO'	RoR/t-bill= 4.10%					
8/21/1970	79.24	78.20	1.31%	B1	78.20					
8/28/1970	81.86	78.64	3.94%							
9/4/1970	82.83	79.14	4.46%							
9/11/1970	82.52	79.55	3.60%							
9/18/1970	82.62	79.92	3.27%							
9/25/1970	83.97	80.40	4.25%							

10/2/1970	85.16	80.97	4.92%				
10/9/1970	85.08	81.46	4.25%				
10/16/1970	84.28	81.80	2.94%				
10/23/1970	83.77	82.04	2.06%				
10/30/1970	83.25	82.19	1.27%				
11/6/1970	84.22	82.44	2.12%				
11/13/1970	83.37	82.56	0.98%				
11/20/1970	83.72	82.70	1.22%				
11/27/1970	85.93	83.09	3.31%				
12/4/1970	89.46	83.85	6.27%				
12/11/1970	90.26	84.61	6.26%				
12/18/1970	90.22	85.28	5.48%				
12/25/1970	90.61	85.92	5.18%				
12/31/1970	92.15	86.66	5.96%	B1'	92.15	rate=	17.84%

Appendix E. S&P 500 Index for 1980

Date - (Friday)	S&P500 Index Price	Y-Process Number	Risk Index (RI)	Ypro buy (B) or sell (S)	Y-Process values		Annual Return (AR)*	Annual Total Return (ATR)**	Year	S&P500 Index ATR % (Bahf)	Y-Process ATR % (Ypro)
1/2/1980	105.76	106.06	-0.29%			ATR		? ATR	80	30.31%	36.53%
1/4/1980	106.52	106.13	0.37%	B0		1980 AR= 25.77%	30.31%	4.54%	81	-4.32%	16.64%
1/11/1980	109.92	106.58	3.04%			1980 FIRM AR= 33.04%	36.53%	3.49%	82	19.64%	36.72%
1/18/1980	111.07	107.12	3.55%			1980 T-Bill= 11.81%	Mkt Risk= 76.92%		83	21.57%	26.30%
1/25/1980	113.61	107.90	5.03%			Div= 4.54%	Rnd Turns=2.0		84	5.90%	16.66%
2/1/1980	115.12	108.76	5.53%	·					85	30.07%	33.47%
2/8/1980	117.95	109.85	6.87%						86	18.04%	22.47%
2/15/1980	115.41	110.52	4.24%						87	5.60%	33.29%
2/22/1980	115.04	111.06	3.46%						88	15.90%	16.53%
2/29/1980	113.66	111.38	2.01%	B0'	111.28	rate= 3.10%			89	30.38%	29.98%
3/7/1980	106.90	110.86	-3.71%	S1						Mkt Risk	Rnd Turns
3/14/1980	105.43	110.23	-4.56%						80	76.92%	Rnd Turns=2.0
3/21/1980	102.31	109.31	-6.84%						81	36.54%	Rnd Turns=5.5
3/28/1980	100.68	108.31	-7.57%						82	48.08%	Rnd Turns=1.5
4/4/1980	102.15	107.59	-5.33%						83	75.00%	Rnd Turns=4.0
4/11/1980	103.79	107.16	-3.24%						84	44.23%	Rnd Turns=4.5
4/18/1980	100.55	106.39	-5.81%						85	80.77%	Rnd Turns=3.0
4/25/1980	105.16	106.25	-1.04%						86	80.77%	Rnd Turns=3.0
5/2/1980	105.58	106.19	-0.57%						87	71.15%	Rnd Turns=2.5
5/9/1980	104.72	106.02	-1.25%	S1'		RoR/t-bill= 2.50%			88	57.69%	Rnd Turns=6.0
5/16/1980	107.35	106.19	1.08%	B1	106.13				89	92.31%	Rnd Turns=2.0
5/23/1980	110.62	106.72	3.52%								
5/30/1980	111.24	107.27	3.57%			AVE ROUND TURNS FOR FOR 80s=				3.4	
6/6/1980	113.20	107.97	4.62%								
6/13/1980	115.81	108.91	5.96%								
6/20/1980	114.06	109.52	3.98%								
6/27/1980	116.00	110.30	4.92%								
7/4/1980	117.46	111.15	5.37%								
7/11/1980	117.84	111.95	5.00%								
7/18/1980	122.04	113.15	7.29%								
7/25/1980	120.78	114.06	5.57%								
8/1/1980	121.21	114.91	5.20%								
8/8/1980	123.61	115.95	6.20%								
8/15/1980	125.72	117.11	6.85%								
8/22/1980	126.02	118.17	6.23%								
8/29/1980	122.38	118.68	3.03%								
9/5/1980	124.88	119.42	4.37%								
9/12/1980	125.54	120.15	4.29%								
9/19/1980	129.25	121.23	6.20%								
9/26/1980	126.35	121.85	3.56%								

10/3/1980	129.33	122.74	5.09%				
10/10/1980	130.29	123.64	5.10%				
10/17/1980	131.52	124.58	5.28%				
10/24/1980	129.85	125.21	3.57%				
10/31/1980	127.47	125.49	1.55%				
11/7/1980	129.18	125.94	2.51%				
11/14/1980	137.15	127.27	7.20%				
11/21/1980	139.11	128.68	7.50%				
11/28/1980	140.52	130.08	7.43%				
12/5/1980	134.03	130.56	2.59%	B1'	130.49	rate=	22.95%
12/12/1980	129.23	130.42	-0.92%	'S2'		RoR/t-bill=	2.95%
12/19/1980	133.70	130.82	2.16%	B2			
12/26/1980	136.57	131.51	3.71%				
12/31/1980	135.76	131.51	3.71%	B2'	135.76	rate=	1.54%

Appendix F. S&P 500 Index for 1990

Date - (Friday)	S&P500 Index Price	Y-Process Number	Risk Index (RI)	Ypro buy (B) or sell (S)	Y-Process values	Annual Return (AR)*	Annual Total Return (ATR)**		Year	S&P500 Index ATR % (Bahf)	Y-Process ATR % (Ypro)
12/31/1989	353.40	345.43	2.25%								
1/5/1990	352.20	346.26	1.69%	B0'	346.01	rate= -2.09%	? ATR	? ATR	90	-2.90%	12.44%
1/12/1990	339.93	345.55	-1.65%	S1		1990 AR= -6.56%	-2.90%	3.66%	91	29.24%	33.76%
1/19/1990	339.15	344.83	-1.68%			1990 FIRM AR= 11.17%	12.44%	1.27%	92	7.30%	8.81%
1/26/1990	325.80	342.63	-5.16%			1990 T-Bill= 7.51%	Mkt Risk = 34.62%		93	9.76%	9.92%
2/2/1990	330.92	341.28	-3.13%			Div= 3.66%	Rnd Turns=5.0		94	1.33%	8.31%
2/9/1990	333.62	340.42	-2.04%						95	36.35%	36.35%
2/16/1990	332.72	339.54	-2.05%						96	22.27%	22.69%
2/23/1990	324.15	337.77	-4.20%						97	32.55%	37.74%
3/2/1990	335.54	337.54	-0.60%	S1'		RoR/t-bill= 1.16%			98	27.85%	34.95%
3/9/1990	337.93	337.62	0.09%	B1			est.=		99	16.82%	20.08%
3/16/1990	341.91	338.16	1.10%	B1'						Mkt Risk	Rnd Turns
3/23/1990	337.22	338.08	-0.26%	S2'		RoR/t-bill= 0.29%			90	34.62%	Rnd Turns=5.0
3/30/1990	339.94	338.33	0.47%	B2	338.17				91	82.69%	Rnd Turns=5.0
4/6/1990	340.08	338.57	0.44%						92	78.85%	Rnd Turns=4.0
4/13/1990	344.34	339.28	1.47%	B2'	339.08	rate= 0.27%			93	88.46%	Rnd Turns=5.0
4/20/1990	335.12	338.83	-1.11%	S2					94	51.92%	Rnd Turns=7.5
4/27/1990	329.11	337.72	-2.62%	S2'		RoR/t-bill= 0.43%			95	100.00%	Rnd Turns=0.5
5/4/1990	338.39	337.83	0.17%	B3	337.84				96	88.46%	Rnd Turns=2.0
5/11/1990	352.00	339.53	3.54%						97	86.54%	Rnd Turns=2.0
5/18/1990	354.64	341.34	3.75%						98	78.85%	Rnd Turns=2.0
5/25/1990	354.58	342.94	3.28%						99	78.85%	Rnd Turns=?
6/1/1990	363.16	345.35	4.90%								
6/8/1990	358.71	346.96	3.28%				AVE ROUND TURNS FOR 90s =			3.8	
6/15/1990	362.91	348.87	3.87%								
6/22/1990	355.43	349.68	1.62%								
6/29/1990	358.02	350.69	2.05%								
7/6/1990	358.42	351.64	1.89%								
7/13/1990	367.31	353.52	3.75%								
7/20/1990	361.61	354.51	1.96%	B3'	354.45	rate= 4.92%					
7/27/1990	353.44	354.42	-0.28%	S1							
8/3/1990	344.86	353.33	-2.46%								
8/10/1990	335.52	351.27	-4.69%								
8/17/1990	327.83	348.54	-6.32%								
8/24/1990	311.51	344.22	-10.50%								
8/31/1990	322.56	341.70	-5.94%								
9/7/1990	323.40	339.58	-5.00%								
9/14/1990	316.83	336.94	-6.35%								
9/21/1990	311.32	333.96	-7.27%								
9/28/1990	306.05	330.71	-8.06%								

10/5/1990	311.50	328.48	-5.45%			
########	300.03	325.16	-8.38%			
########	312.48	323.70	-3.59%			
########	304.71	321.50	-5.51%			
11/2/1990	311.85	320.40	-2.74%			
11/9/1990	313.74	319.64	-1.88%			
########	317.12	319.38	-0.71%			
########	315.10	318.91	-1.21%	S1'		RoR/t-bill= 2.74%
########	322.22	319.33	0.90%	B4	319.19	
12/7/1990	327.75	320.35	2.26%			
########	326.82	321.15	1.74%			
########	331.75	322.43	2.81%			
########	328.72	323.20	1.68%			
########	330.22	324.06	1.87%	B4'		rate= 3.46%

Get 13 Free Weeks of the
Y-PROCESS ® NEWSLETTER

USE THE Y-PROCESS® TO BUILD AND MANAGE YOUR OWN PORTFOLIO.

PROTECT YOUR EQUITY FROM STOCK MARKET DOWN TURNS. KNOW WHEN TO GET IN & OUT OF THE MARKET.

SUBSCRIBE TO THE Y-PROCESS ® NEWSLETTER TODAY.

Please fill out the form on the reverse side, cut out this page, fold, tape & mail, or fax to : 1-856-424-1975.

- Fold Here -

Y-PROCESS® NEWSLETTER
YANIS FINANCIAL SERVICES, INC.
35 Cooper Run Drive
Cherry Hill, NJ 08003-2244

Y-PROCESS® NEWSLETTER

FREE 13 WEEK subscription to the Y-Process® newsletter, with the buy, sell and hold numbers of key stock market indexes, mutual funds and stocks. Build your own equity portfolio the easy way — use the Y-Process® model — described in *Dancing With Bears*©, the best stock market-timing book available today. Get on track and create extraordinary wealth the Y-Process® way. Learn more about how to obtain stock market security by visiting our website <www.yprocess.com> for more information about the Yanis Financial Service, Inc. and our weekly newsletter.

At the end of the 13 weeks you will be billed for a 1 year subscription at the low price of $3.80/week ($197.60/year). You may pay for your subscription on our secure website with a Visa, Master Card, American Express or Discover Card, or by sending your payment by US Mail using a credit card, personal check or money order.

If you do not have internet access you can receive the 13 week newsletter free via US Mail* or fax.

*Newsletters sent by US Mail are subject to the speed of the US Mail delivery service.

--Fold Here--

Y-PROCESS ® NEWSLETTER

☐ **YES,** sign me up for my Free 13 weekly issues (for new clients only) of the Y-Process® Newsletter (a $49.40 value).

Mr/Ms/Mrs : _____

Address: _____

City/State/Zip: _____

Email: _____ Fax: _____

Tele.#: Day ( )_____ Eve.: ( )_____

I will receive via email my password & ID # for my personal website access.

☐ I do not have Internet access. I would like my subscription ☐ mailed or ☐ faxed to me.

For Office Use Only ☐☐☐☐☐☐